W9-DGS-431

Ethnic
Awareness .
and the School

SAGE SERIES ON RACE AND ETHNIC RELATIONS

Series Editor:
JOHN H. STANFIELD II
College of William and Mary

This series is designed for scholars working in creative theoretical areas related to race and ethnic relations. The series will publish books and collections of original articles that critically assess and expand upon race and ethnic relations issues from American and comparative points of view.

SERIES EDITORIAL BOARD

Robert Blauner	William Liu
Jomills H. Braddock II	Stanford M. Lyman
Scott Cummings	Gary Marx
Rutledge Dennis	Robert Miles
Leonard Dinnerstein	Rebecca Morales
Reynolds Farley	Chester Pierce
Joe Feagin	Vicki L. Ruiz
Barry Glassner	Gary D. Sandefur
Ruth S. Hamilton	Diana Slaughter
Dell Hymes	C. Matthew Snipp
James Jackson	John Stone
Roy Bryce Laporte	Bruce Williams
Paul Gordon Lauren	Melvin D. Williams

Volumes in this series include

1. Roger Waldinger, Howard Aldrich, Robin Ward, and Associates, ETHNIC ENTREPRENEURS: Immigrant Business in Industrial Societies
2. Philomena Essed, UNDERSTANDING EVERYDAY RACISM: An Interdisciplinary Theory
3. Samuel V. Duh, BLACKS AND AIDS: Causes and Origins
4. Steven J. Gold, REFUGEE COMMUNITIES: A Comparative Field Study
5. Mary E. Andereck, ETHNIC AWARENESS AND THE SCHOOL: An Ethnographic Study

Ethnic Awareness and the School

An Ethnographic Study

Mary E. Andereck

Foreword by ANDREW M. GREELEY

Sage Series on Race and Ethnic Relations
v o l u m e   5

SAGE Publications
International Educational and Professional Publisher
Newbury Park   London   New Delhi

Copyright © 1992 by Sage Publications, Inc.

All rights reserved. No part of this book may be reproduced or utilized in any form or by any means, electronic or mechanical, including photocopying, recording, or by any information storage and retrieval system, without permission in writing from the publisher.

For information address:

SAGE Publications, Inc.
2455 Teller Road
Newbury Park, California 91320

SAGE Publications Ltd.
6 Bonhill Street
London EC2A 4PU
United Kingdom

SAGE Publications India Pvt. Ltd.
M-32 Market
Greater Kailash I
New Delhi 110 048 India

Printed in the United States of America

Library of Congress Cataloging-in-Publication Data

Andereck, Mary E.
    Ethnic awareness and the school: an ethnographic study / Mary E. Andereck; foreword by Andrew M. Greeley.
        p.   cm.—(Sage series on race and ethnic relations; v. 5)
    Includes bibliographical references (p.   ) and index.
    ISBN 0-8039-3886-1.—ISBN 0-8039-3887-X (pbk.)
    1. Irish Travelers (Nomadic people)—Education—Alabama—Case studies.   2. Catholic elementary schools—Alabama—Case studies.
3. Ethnic attitudes—Alabama—Case studies.   I. Title.   II. Series.
LC36.50I74A53   1992
305.8—dc20   91-44223
                                                              CIP

92 93 94 95   10 9 8 7 6 5 4 3 2 1

Sage Production Editor: Chiara C. Huddleston

LIBRARY
ALMA COLLEGE
ALMA, MICHIGAN

For Skeeter, Shea, and Grace
and
in memory of Seuwannee

Contents

Acknowledgments

I wish to thank all those at "St. Jude School" and my family and friends who directly or indirectly provided encouragement and support for this book. The Irish Travelers interviewed and observed for this book are anonymous but, to these unnamed collaborators, I wish to express my profound admiration and gratitude.

Foreword

In my early years in the priesthood, long before I became a sociologist or even thought of visiting Ireland, I read an article in *The New York Times* (I guess I was an elitist even then) about a community of "Irish Travelers" in the southern part of the United States, a community that was centered in a place in northern Alabama, which, as I remember, was called "Priest's Corner." I was fascinated by the fact that a small group of families could maintain their distinctive culture in an environment that was not only hostile (as was their environment in their native Ireland) but foreign, and, being in the southern United States, utterly foreign. How could they do it, I wondered.

It was a question that bothered me in later years after I had become a sociologist and indeed one who specialized in the study of ethnic subcultures. I acquired, because of that *New York Times* article, an interest in "pariah" cultures and especially in the "Gypsies," or Rom as they call themselves, a house of which, it turned out, we had in our upper-middle-class Irish parish on the fringes of Chicago. Reading the literature on the Rom made me feel sympathetic toward them and even admire them.

The Irish Travelers in the old country, I would learn on subsequent visits, were Celts, although their pariah subculture was in many respects like that of the Rom and an occasional Romany word had found its way into their patois. They were cordially disliked by most Irishmen just as the Gypsies were disliked by most Americans.

My friend Eammon Casey, Bishop of Galway and Kilmacduff (and Apostolic Administrator of Kilfenora!), was a champion of the "itinerants" or "tinkers" as the Irish called them and brought me to some of the shelters he had constructed for them. Their children swarmed around Eammon, knowing a friend and a protector when they saw one, and around me, figuring that a friend of their friend was a friend of theirs.

The Travelers, like the Rom, are essentially gentle people (though, unlike the Rom, they are not by principle and religion nonviolent). They may steal and lie to survive, but they do no great harm to anyone. They are hated because they are an outcast people whom the larger society can turn into an inkblot for their fears and hostilities.

I wondered in Ireland as I had after reading the *The New York Times* article how such subcultures survive enormous pressures toward assimilation. Their lives would be much happier, would they not, if they became like all the rest of us?

So, when I was asked to read Dr. Andereck's book, I jumped at the opportunity. Perhaps I would find an explanation. I was not disappointed. It is the enormous merit of this study that it establishes in precise and elaborate detail how the Travelers and the non-Travelers go about setting up ethnic group boundaries—and note that most of the non-Travelers are also Irish American Catholics living in the larger, somewhat hostile (to Catholics) culture of the U.S. South.

It would be difficult to overestimate the importance of Dr. Andereck's achievement. The reader will learn both about one of the more fascinating small ethnic groups in America and about the dynamics of ethnic boundary establishment among children in elementary school.

The question remains, as it always does in books on ethnicity, about whether assimilation might not be "better" for the Travelers. Then they could go to colleges and graduate schools like the rest of us (and read *The New York Times*!).

(I asked Bishop Casey whether he was ever able to send one of his Travelers to university. No, he replied, but he did get one into nurse's training. He shrugged. She became pregnant before she finished her course.)

I am not a cultural relativist. Some cultures are better than others. Some impose constraints that limit the growth of the human spirit. Pariah people suffer for their outcast status. One cannot help feel sorry for the Travelers as one reads this book.

It is not, however, cultural relativism to say that some cultures that are in many ways inferior are also in some ways superior. Perhaps the Travelers understand something about the meaning and purpose of life and the importance of loyalty to family and friends that the rest of us have forgotten. In any case, it is *their* culture and, if they want to preserve it, it is their right to do so in a pluralistic society like ours—and in Ireland too. (Conor Ward and I have recently demonstrated in an analysis of the International Study of Values that, on a nine-item scale of measure of tolerance, Ireland is the most tolerant country in the English-speaking world.)

The appropriate stance, it seems to me, toward groups like the Travelers is to respect their right to be who and what they are and to listen to them with generosity and openness to see what we might learn from them.

Andrew M. Greeley
National Opinion Research Center

1

Introduction

This chapter is a discussion of the limitations in the field of ethnic studies on ethnic groups that have chosen to accommodate rather than acculturate or assimilate. A distinction must be made between the three terms. *Assimilation* is the total absorption of one culture into another, so that the first no longer has defining characteristics (Theodorson and Theodorson 1969, p. 17). *Acculturation* is a term often defined using the term *accommodation,* although the two terms are not synonymous. *Acculturation* is the gradual movement of a group or individual toward assimilation, with assimilation being the final product. *Accommodation* refers to the process by which a group alters any behaviors or values that are strongly antagonistic to the dominant group in hopes of maintaining group cohesiveness (Theodorson and Theodorson 1969, p. 3). These changes are minimal and are not perceived as threatening to the group's identity. Accommodation is a process of alteration but should not be interpreted as moving toward assimilation. Accommodating groups have very strong boundary rules that contribute to the reduced chance of acculturating or assimilating.

Every ethnic group has boundary rules to maintain ethnicity. One way to understand the importance of a group's ethnicity is to study boundary rules that are seen in the interaction patterns between the ethnic group and the nonethnic group. To be a member of an ethnic group, one must show "overt signals or signs" advocated by the group (Barth 1969, p. 14). Without outward signs of ethnicity displayed to nonmembers, the group risks losing its identity. The construction of these overt signs of ethnicity are influenced by the responses by nonmembers. If the overt signs are the same as those practiced by nonmembers, then the ethnic group identity is threatened.

Identifying criteria reinforced with boundary rules are necessary to maintain members. Differing values or beliefs must be converted into actions that represent these ideas and, as important, outsiders must also interpret these ideas as different than their own.

The interaction between members of an ethnic group and nonmembers may easily be analyzed in a large social organization such as a school. The school setting is an important one for studying an ethnic group's desires for maintaining its ethnicity. The school is often identified as one of the most important socializing agents of society, sometimes replacing the family and the church. When an ethnic group enrolls its children in the schools, it risks losing some of its socializing power.

Through school experiences, U.S. children are exposed to ethnic groups with whom they have not interacted as closely in any other social situation. Family members may not be ethnically diverse and neither may their neighborhood or church. Up until school age, most U.S. children, regardless of ethnicity, have had only brief encounters with members of an ethnic group other than their own. Even with increasing enrollment in day-care centers, children are still divided by such factors as economics and/or neighborhoods. Economics, in general, in the South, continues to be racially and ethnically based. Although the child in day care has a better chance of broader experience with other ethnic groups than the child who remains at home, recognition of ethnic constancy may not develop until the child reaches age 7 or 8 (Aboud 1987). The first stage that approaches ethnic awareness is self-awareness, generally occurring at 3 or 4 years of age (Aboud 1987). Day-care-age children, no matter how diverse their backgrounds, may not be developmentally ready to recognize ethnic differences. Not until the children are in elementary school are they developmentally ready to classify and label individuals into ethnic and racial groups (Aboud 1987).

This book focuses on the influence that one Catholic school, in the southern United States, has on a small cultural enclave of people, called Irish Travelers, and the influence the Irish Travelers have on the Catholic school.

Irish Travelers compose a small itinerant ethnic group, often referred to, incorrectly, as "Irish Gypsies." Irish Travelers have resided primarily in the South for more than 140 years (Andereck 1988). Originally horse and mule traders, Irish Travelers now earn their living traveling for the majority of the year, spraypainting, asphalting, or laying linoleum. Brought together by the development of ethnic communalities over time and the practice of itinerant occupations, Irish Travelers have formed a distinct ethnic group with a complex set of boundary rules to maintain this ethnicity.

Irish Travelers fit the description of an accommodating ethnic group. For 140 years, they have maintained their distinctiveness by "accommodating" to the surrounding culture but not "giving in." Other more known groups that follow the same process of ethnicity are Gypsies and the Amish.

The research field of ethnicity often ignores the accommodating groups and, as a result, public policy, especially in the field of formal education, often does not incorporate the needs or desires of these groups.

Irish Travelers in the United States have not been subjects of research in the educational field. Using this ethnic group as an example of an accommodating group for this book, I am able to present my theories of the development of ethnic attitudes and behaviors among school-aged children and the sources of influence of these attitudes and behavior. In my research, I was able to observe the consequences of an accommodating rather than an acculturating group entering an institution of formal education set up by the dominant group. This information is important because of the fact that school personnel are trained to deal with acculturating groups rather than accommodating groups. The research required the use of ethnography (participant observation and in-depth interviewing over time) in the classroom and in the community.

All place names and personal names have been changed. Newspaper articles have not been referenced in the bibliography but instead cited as "southern newspapers" in the text. These decisions were made to protect all those involved in the study. I had guaranteed anonymity to all Travelers and non-Travelers at the targeted school, which has been renamed "St. Jude." The requests of all have been met through these changes.

2

Ethnic Groups and Ethnicity

ETHNIC GROUPS

The existence of ethnic diversity in U.S. society is well documented, although the basic definition of *ethnicity* is ambiguous. The U.S. Bureau of the Census uses the term *race* without defining the categories, such as White, Black or Negro, Indian (American), and nine racial groups of Asian or Pacific Islanders with the opportunity to write in "other" for race (U.S. Bureau of the Census, 1990). The person completing the census survey is asked to choose the category with which he or she identifies—socially or psychologically. Questions about ancestry or ethnic origin are also asked in the census, again asking the person completing the survey to chose only one ethnic origin. In 1960, "Hispanic" was identified by the U.S. government as a race, as were White and Black, although it is a very broad cultural classification. The confusion of racial and ethnic categories was an influential factor in changing the census in 1980 to specify 14 race categories instead of 8 as in 1970. Currently, Hispanic peoples are more easily identified through a Spanish surname question and the questions dealing with ancestry and parents' place of birth. The Census Bureau makes note that "Spanish origin is not a race category, and persons of Spanish origin may be of any race" (U.S. Bureau of the Census, 1982, p. 38).

The term *ethnic group,* used by many social science researchers, is often used without explanation. Isajiw (1974, p. 11) reviewed 65 sources on ethnic research and found that 52 sources did not define the terms *ethnicity* or *ethnic groups* although they were used throughout the book or article. Of the 65 studies reviewed, 12 defined one or two of the terms, describing such characteristics as common ancestral origin, same culture, religion, language, gemeinschaft type of relations, and immigrant background. Isajiw found that the definitions examined differed greatly in regard to which characteristics were included and which were excluded (Isajiw 1974, p. 117).

Without clear definitions of the terms *race* or *ethnic group,* interpretations of the terms are unlimited, as Isajiw (1974) found in his research. There continue to be various definitions for *ethnic group* and related terms in the literature. For example, Francis (1976, p. 6) states, "Certain people are socially defined as belonging together by virtue of common descent. Ethnicity may be said to be dominant if it is salient in the orientation of social action." Rotheram and Phinney (1987, p. 12) write that an ethnic group is "any collection of people who call themselves an ethnic group and who see themselves sharing common attributes. Being a minority in numbers and/or status is not a prerequisite."

Martin and Franklin (1973, p. 26) state, "Social taxonomy," or classifying individuals into groups, "is not an exact science; we are confronted with such problems as whether or not to recognize the person's own classification as valid or to consider his classification by others as authoritative." With such a problem, comparative analysis of social behavior patterns of ethnic or racial groups may be invalid. A researcher may be comparing two groups that are not truly similar; such may be the case with accommodating groups and acculturating groups.

For this study, the definition of *ethnicity* must include "overt features and values" identified by others through interaction, as described by Royce (1982):

> An "ethnic group" is a reference group invoked by people who share a common historical style (which may be only assumed), based on overt features and values, and who, through the process of interaction with others identify themselves as sharing that style. "Ethnic identity" is the sum total of feelings on the part of group members about those values, symbols, and common histories, that identify them as a distinct group. "Ethnicity" is simply ethnic-based action. (Royce 1982, pp. 17-18)

There are different categories of ethnic groups in U.S. society. The categorization of ethnic group types is dependent upon the social conditions experienced by the group. For example, there are a number of combinations of variables that describe the social conditions surrounding an ethnic group: time period entering the United States, religion, race, economics, language, group's reaction to the host country, geographic residence in the host country, and occupational skills. Mindel and Habenstein (1978), Greeley (1974, 1977), and Gordon (1964) have written extensively in the field of ethnicity but their perspectives for analyzing the ethnic experience differs substantively. I will discuss Greeley's (1974, 1977) perspectives after the other two because of his description of so many perspectives.

Mindel and Habenstein (1978) grouped ethnic families into four categories influenced by sociohistorical circumstances: (a) early-arriving ethnic minorities (in the United States for 75-100 years), such as Polish, Japanese, Irish, Chinese, and Italians; (b) recent and continuing ethnic minorities (late 1800s and early 1900s), such as Arabs, Greeks, and Puerto Ricans; (c) historically subjugated but volatile ethnic minorities, such as Blacks, Native Americans, and Latins; and (d) socioreligious ethnic groups, such as Amish, Jews, and Mormons. Mindel and Habenstein's categories are not absolute (i.e., an ethnic group may fall within two or more categories). The categories do consider the importance of history within the host country, but, as in Greeley's perspective explained below, the history of the group within its own country is important also.

Gordon (1964, p. 174) differs from Mindel and Habenstein and Greeley in that he focuses on the aspects of the assimilation process:

1. Cultural Assimilation (or acculturation)—change of cultural patterns to those of the host society.
2. Structural Assimilation—large scale entrance into clubs and institutions of host society on the primary group level.
3. Marital Society—large scale intermarriage or amalgamation.
4. Identificational Assimilation—development of sense of peoplehood based exclusively on the host society.
5. Attitude Receptional Assimilation—absence of prejudice.
6. Behavior Receptional Assimilation—absence of discrimination.
7. Absence of Value and Power Conflict—civic assimilation.

The existence of all seven subprocesses represents Gordon's "ideal type" of assimilation. A group that has not assimilated into the dominant group, however, may experience one or a combination of the assimilation variables. In defining the term *ethnic group*, one must consider the particular stage that best describes the group in relation to total assimilation. The definition must be broad enough to include any group at any stage of the assimilation process. Gordon's model assumes, however, that an ethnic group is on the path toward assimilation and it does not take into account the process of accommodation.

Greeley (1974, 1977) presents four common perspectives in the literature of ethnicity: the Anglo Conformity perspective, the Melting Pot perspective, the Cultural Pluralism perspective, and the Acculturation-Assimilation perspective. He then explains his perspective, which he calls Ethnogenesis.

The Anglo Conformity perspective is made up of separate host and immigrant cultures. Over time, the immigrant becomes more like the host and finally assimilates into the host culture. Greeley sees a limitation in the perspective. The continuation of a different immigrant culture after the fourth generation cannot be explained through the Anglo Conformity perspective (Greeley 1977, p. 23).

The Melting Pot perspective refers to a combination of characteristics of both the host and the immigrant cultures into one culture. Even with a sharing of cultures, the amount of sharing by either side is difficult to measure.

The Cultural Pluralism perspective suggests that the immigrant accepts some of the host culture for functional reasons but the society continues to maintain separate culture systems.

The Acculturation-Assimilation perspective is taken from Milton Gordon (1964); it suggests a sharing between host and immigrant but immigrants still retaining cultural traits that "distinguish host from immigrant" (Greeley 1974, p. 306), although not to the extreme of Cultural Pluralism.

The Ethnogenesis perspective is Greeley's extension of the Acculturation-Assimilation perspective. What Greeley (1974, p. 310) sees as lacking in the other four perspectives is the influence of an "immigrant groups' experiencial [*sic*] history in this country and in the country of origin toward the creation of distinct cultural systems."

Greeley's ethnicization perspective does describe the development of Irish Travelers in the United States, but it does not explain the process of accommodation over generations and the role of conflict in maintaining ethnicity.

Modern-day ethnicity in the United States is a cultural phenomena rather than a biological phenomena. Humans define ethnic boundaries and act upon these boundaries. Because of this, if two groups interact (one assumed to be ethnic and the other nonethnic) but ethnicity is not identifiable by the nonethnics, then ethnicity is not "real" (e.g., a person may believe he is a member of an ethnic group but, until others act upon his said ethnicity, he is not truly an ethnic). My theory that ethnicity is a result of interaction best suits the perspective of symbolic interaction and its three basic assumptions: (a) Social reality is a social production; (b) humans are capable of shaping and guiding their own behavior; and (c) while shaping and guiding their own behavior, humans interact with others. This interaction influences how humans define themselves and others around them. If humans define reality through interaction, then humans also define ethnicity through interaction: "Humans learn their basic symbols, their conceptions of self, and the definitions they attach to social objects through interaction with others" (Denzin 1978, p. 7).

ETHNIC SOCIALIZATION AND ETHNIC IDENTITY

The interaction process contributes to the development of one's ethnic awareness, and interaction and socialization begin in childhood. This learning process is referred to as "ethnic socialization." Specifically, "ethnic socialization refers to the developmental processes by which children acquire the behaviors, perceptions, values, and attitudes of an ethnic group, and come to see themselves and others as members of such groups" (Phinney and Rotheram 1987, p. 11).

Ethnic identity is an important concept in analyzing ethnic socialization. *Ethnic identity,* although a broad term, is formed from a child's ethnic socialization. Ethnic identity may include ethnic awareness, ethnic self-identification, ethnic attitudes, and ethnic behaviors

(Rotheram and Phinney 1987, p. 13), but ethnic socialization focuses on the development of an ethnic identity.

There are numerous theorists who focus on cognitive development, but Rotheram and Phinney (1987, p. 15) present four interesting theories of the stages of development of ethnic and racial attitudes proposed by the following researchers: Goodman (1964), Porter (1971), Katz (1976), and Aboud (1977).

Goodman (1964) presents three stages of ethnic development: (a) ethnic awareness, ages 3 to 4; (b) ethnic orientation, ages 4 to 8; and (c) attitude crystallization, ages 8 to 10. Goodman focuses his stages on ethnic rather than racial concepts and attitudes.

Porter (1971) found that children develop attitudes at a much earlier age when race rather than ethnicity is the focus. He presents three stages for the development of racial concepts and attitudes: (a) awareness of color differences by age 3, (b) incipient racial attitudes by age 4, and (c) strong social preferences with reasons by age 5. Porter (1971) found that, by 4 years of age, children are developing racial attitudes and, by age 5, hold strong social preferences with reasons for these preferences. A number of empirical studies have found similar results, suggesting that racial attitudes due to the salience of skin color develop much earlier among children than do attitudes toward ethnic groups. Members of ethnic groups may be more difficult to identify by children due to the more complex characteristics of ethnicity.

According to Katz (1976), children observe cues between 0 and 3 years of age and, between 1 and 4 years, they form rudimentary concepts. Within this three-year period, children begin to develop conceptual differentiation and recognize the irrevocability of cues. By ages 5 to 7, children are able to consolidate group concepts and increase their perceptual and cognitive abilities. As these developmental processes occur, attitudes are crystallized between 8 and 10 years of age.

Aboud (1977) provides a general sequential theory development of ethnic socialization that does not use age categories: (a) unawareness of ethnic affiliation, (b) awareness of groups leading to social comparison, (c) awareness of group affiliation, and (d) curiosity about other groups. Aboud believes racial groups are also identified through these same stages, although the movement from one stage to another may be at an earlier age. Aboud also states that children have a number of influences that play a role in their development, and age alone may not predict at which stage a child may develop ethnic or racial concepts and attitudes.

These studies conclude that children entering school at kindergarten age have preconceived ethnic and racial attitudes. Of course, these attitudes may change for the better or for the worse in the school setting over the years, but most children by age 10, or fifth grade, have well-developed racial and ethnic attitudes.

Goodman (1964), Porter (1971), Katz (1976), and Aboud (1977) have provided generalizations in their theories of the development of ethnic identity, but the extent of ethnic awareness and attitudes is dependent upon the group in which the child belongs. For example, minority children tend to develop race awareness earlier than nonminority children (Clark and Clark 1939; Goodman 1964).

Landreth and Johnson (1953, p. 78) found in their study of Black children that "patterns of response to persons of different skin color are present as early as three years and become accentuated during the succeeding two years."

Ethnic or racial awareness precedes attitudes and preference for one's own or another group. Preference for one's own group differs between White and Black children. White children prefer to play with Whites by the age of 4 years (Asher and Allen 1969; Clark, Hocevar, and Dembo 1980; Hraba and Grant 1970; Kircher and Furby 1971; Williams et al. 1975). Research results differ in reporting own-group preference after 6 or 7 years of age. Rice, Ruiz, and Padilla (1974) and Zinser, Rich, and Bailey (1981) found a decrease in own-group preferences among White children, while Aboud (1977), Epstein, Krupat, and Obudho (1976), Fox and Jordan (1973), Genessee, Tucker, and Lambert (1978), and George and Hoppe (1979) found no change in own-group preference during these years.

Some Black children at 3 to 4 years of age tend to prefer other Blacks over Whites, but the largest percentage of Black children had no preference (Aboud 1984, p. 7). Among other minorities, preschool Chinese Canadians and 5- to 7-year-old Chinese Americans showed no preference for their own group (Aboud 1977; Fox and

Jordan 1973). A significant proportion of Native Americans at 5 and 6 years preferred and positively evaluated Whites.

From all the studies mentioned above, racial and ethnic awareness is dependent upon the type of group in which the child belongs. Although the type of group plays a vital role in perceptions, the measurement tool by which a researcher collects data must also be analyzed. Many of the research studies of children's ethnic or racial preference have used dolls or pictures. Clark and Clark, in 1947, initiated the preference task using Black and White dolls. The child was asked to choose the nice doll, the pretty doll, and so on. The administration of the preference test was easily adapted to other studies. The Clarks' research results were significant in the Kansas Supreme Court decision to ban school segregation in 1954 (*Brown v. the Topeka Board of Education*; Katz 1976, p. 127).

The doll or picture preference measure has been criticized on the basis that the researcher uses the doll or picture as an example of a race or ethnic group. The child is expected to observe and then base his or her choice on the critical attributes that distinguish one ethnic or racial member from another (Phinney and Rotheram 1987, p. 19). This forced choice methodology ignores analysis of a child's choice. The testers, if they do not ask the children why they chose a particular doll or picture, may assume reasons that do not coincide with the children's reasons. "Although affective processes often influence what children remember and integrate from various experiences, their level of cognitive development determines the ways in which they process that information" (Ramsey 1987, p. 72). Beyond level of cognitive development, children do have varying reasons for choices that are not easily identified by adults without deeper probing.

During what Piaget (1954) would identify as the concrete stage, children's level of cognitive ability inhibits the interpretation of their responses using adult criteria. Children do not process information on ethnicity in the same way that adults do. Problems of reliability and validity have not been solved in using doll and picture choice measures of racial and ethnic attitudes. Numerous studies suggest that nursery school children respond in the way they believe the examiner expects them to respond (Stevenson and Stevenson 1960; Hraba and Grant 1970; and Porter 1971). More recent research, however, has shown that, due to the fact that children have more interaction with testers, the race of the tester is not as important a factor as gender continues to be (Spencer 1984). Participant observation has shown that children's choices on a doll measure do not correlate with behavior in a natural setting such as a playground. Children may be answering preference tests based on the item used rather than transferring the questions to "real life." By this I mean that children, when asked, "Which is the nice lady?" may be answering the question based on the dolls or pictures rather than using the racial characteristics and applying them to their attitudes toward racial groups on the playground or on the street.

There have been a number of researchers who have used the doll and picture tests in the 1980s to determine whether Black children had developed more of a Black preference than Black children of the 1950s and 1960s (Fine and Bowers 1984; Mays 1986; Powell-Hopson and Hopson 1988). Spencer (1982, 1984, 1985) has done numerous studies on the race preference of Black children using doll and picture tests with the additional qualitative methods of participant observation and in-depth interviewing. She has concluded that preschool Black children holding White-biased racial attitudes and preferences do not necessarily internalize the beliefs because they are at the preoperational stage of development. Not until they move into the concrete operational stage will they be more likely to internalize their race preferences.

Although there are problems with preference tests, and possible ways to combat the problems, the best way to study an ethnic group is when it is interacting with nonmembers. Rotheram and Phinney (1987, p. 25) have found six different perspectives on the study of ethnic socialization: (a) the level at which the topic is analyzed (child, family, community, society); (b) the viewpoint adopted (observer versus child); (c) assumptions regarding change (developmental processes, group processes, or secular trends); (d) methodology used; (e) groups studied; and (f) goals of the research.

The assumptions regarding a change in children's ethnic socialization have often been analyzed from a developmental approach because of the influence of Piaget's theories of child development. Due to the impact of theories of cognitive developmentalists on the school setting (e.g., grades by age rather than by ability), this study focuses on the school experiences based on grade level. Although cognitive development theories may not be the best to explain the ethnic socialization of accommodating groups such as Irish Travelers, the theories have been empirically based in the literature in analyzing the development of ethnic identity in children (Rotheram and Phinney 1987).

The cognitive development perspective of grouping children by age may limit some children's further development, suggesting that the labeling of children into grades, which includes expected cognitive knowledge attained, may encourage children to act out only those expected behaviors. The same process may occur for ethnic development. The schools limit the knowledge for each grade level and, as a result, one's ethnic development may also be limited.

The teaching styles, learning styles, and classroom structures that are the focus of research on educating minority students do not appear to be significant factors in the academic or social achievement of accommodating ethnic students. Awareness of the learning styles of groups such as Native Americans and Asian Americans has contributed to an increase in these groups' academic successes; however, for accommodating groups, with their differing values toward formal education, school changes or adaptations have not been influential in changing their academic expectations or experiences.

The major difference that researchers must be aware of when generalizing about ethnic/minority groups is that accommodating groups do exist in the schools and the schools are instructed to deal with these students in the same ways as they do other racial and ethnic groups. Accommodating ethnic groups are not willing to allow the schools to be more of a socializing agent than the family. This strong belief held by accommodating groups provides some interesting insight into our educational system and our social structure in addition to providing valuable information for a better understanding of ethnicity.

3

Irish Travelers in the United States

GENERAL CHARACTERISTICS

Irish Travelers constitute a small itinerant ethnic group that has resided primarily in the South for more than 100 years (Andereck 1988). Originally horse and mule traders, Irish Travelers now earn their living traveling for the majority of the year, spraypainting, asphalting, or laying linoleum. Irish Travelers are identified by non-Travelers as *Irish Gypsies* due to their itinerant life-styles, although Travelers consider the term a derogatory one.

Irish Travelers divide themselves into three groups based on historical residence: Georgia Travelers, Mississippi Travelers, and Texas Travelers. There is a group called "Ohio Travelers" but these migrated to the Midwest in the late 1800s while other Irish Travelers moved south. Contact between the Ohio Travelers and the Travelers in the southern United States is minimal.

Population figures on Irish Travelers in the United States are unknown. The U.S. Census does not recognize Irish Travelers as a unique ethnic group. The amount of itinerancy and the level of secrecy of the group make enumeration very difficult. According to my research and the Irish Travelers' estimates, the Georgia Travelers' camp is made up of approximately 500 families, the Mississippi Travelers have approximately 200 families, and the Texas Travelers have fewer than 50 families. Irish Traveler families have an average of two or three children.

Irish Travelers in the United States speak English and an argot they call their Cant. Cant is a combination of Shelta, derived from Irish Gaelic, Romanes (the language of Romany gypsies), and English. Travelers use their Cant between themselves in the presence of non-Travelers. Irish Travelers residing in Ireland also speak a similar

Cant but, in the United States, the Cant, over generations, has developed into more of a pidgin English (Harper 1969, 1977). Young Travelers are not as fluent as previous generations and often know only a few phrases or words.

Origin

Personal interviews and the research literature suggest that unstable conditions in Ireland's history, as early as 1641, caused a large percentage of the Irish population to leave their homes in search of food and work. Due to necessity, Irish families took up itinerant occupations such as tinsmithing, horse trading, and selling home-made crafts. The itinerant workers in Ireland and England were referred to as "tinkers"—a name still used in Ireland by the settled population, although it was and continues to be very derogatory (Ranking 1891; Gmelch 1975; personal interviews 1985-91). *Irish Travelers* has slowly become an acceptable reference term.

Irish Travelers in Ireland have been victims of discrimination for years due to their itinerant life-styles (Gmelch 1975). Travelers still may be seen today camping in roadside parks, occasionally in barrel-shaped wagons pulled by horses or mules, as in the past, but usually in automobiles and travel trailers.

Anthropologists George and Sharon Gmelch (S. Gmelch 1975; G. Gmelch 1985) have conducted extensive ethnographic research on Irish Travelers. They have found that the settled Irish population is very prejudiced toward Travelers and act upon generalizations of the group developed from limited interaction.

The *Report of the Commission on Itinerancy* in 1963 revealed the Travelers "as a neglected and impoverished people. This image was reinforced by the Itinerant Settlement Movement which dwelt on the plight of travelers, their poor health, high infant mortality and illiteracy, in an effort to evoke compassion in the settled community and gain support for settlement policies" (Gmelch 1975, p. 7).

The Irish government believed the Itinerant Settlement Movement would give Travelers a chance to receive health care, enroll their children in school, and begin assimilating into the dominant society. The inexpensive housing settlements constructed throughout Ireland

and additional opportunities provided by the government were not always accepted by Travelers. Non-Travelers complained about the housing sites and Traveler children in their schools. Discrimination continued toward Travelers but was felt even more strongly with Travelers living in such close proximity to non-Travelers. Traveler families often paid for their rent at a site although they continued to have a seminomadic life-style. Loneliness and boredom were and still are the two major reasons Travelers return to the road in Ireland (Gmelch 1975).

The continuation of itinerancy reinforces stereotypes. As Gmelch (1975, p. 128) writes, "Not only are they readily identifiable, but there is much less incentive to try to 'pass' when in the sole company of other travelers. Thus before an individual can hope to lose his stigmatized identity, he must abandon his nomadic lifestyle."

One Irish Traveler in Ireland stated:

> People always find out you're travellers. It must be the way travellers dress. And if it's not, it's the way they speak, the way they go on—their movements. It seems to be their walk. You'd nearly know a traveller. If they're dressed in satin and if they had all the gold hangin' out of them, you'd know they were a traveller. You never can hide it. Whatever's in it, you can't hide it. (Gmelch 1975, p. 130)

According to oral history, Irish Travelers in the United States believe there were eight families that independently emigrated from Ireland or England to the United States in the mid-1800s. Traveler families spread throughout the urban areas of the Northeast, practicing itinerant occupations such as tinsmithing and peddling various goods but gradually entered the mule trading business. Many Irish itinerants in Ireland were horse and mule traders, so the occupation was not new to the Irish Travelers in the United States. Irish Travelers increased their numbers by marrying other Irish itinerants in the mule business and, more rarely, Romany gypsies they encountered in their travels.

Before the Civil War, Irish Travelers began trading in the southern states because of the continual use of horse and mule power on southern farms. Irish Travelers would spend winters in the South, trading horses and mules, and return to the North for the warmer

months. As the need for horse and mule power decreased in the North
but continued in the South, Irish Travelers began to set up their home
bases in Nashville, Tennessee, and later Atlanta, Georgia, where the
Irish Travelers began using the label "Georgia Travelers." Once in
Georgia, Irish Travelers began to migrate to other areas of the South.
A group of families moved to Mississippi for economic reasons and
were then called "Mississippi Travelers." The two groups, Georgia
Travelers and Mississippi Travelers, consisted of families that worked
different stock centers. Communication and interaction between the
two groups was and still is constant. A third group, Texas Travelers,
has since emerged and is composed of both Georgia Traveler and
Mississippi Traveler families that became interested in asphalting.
Moving to Texas allowed them to peddle their business to the
growing urban areas affected by the oil boom of the 1970s.

Prior to the 1930s, Irish Travelers moved throughout the Northeast
and South in horse-drawn barrel-shaped wagons as were used by
Irish Travelers in Ireland. With the increased use of automobiles by
the general population, Irish Travelers began using trucks after 1927
and camping in large tents with wooden floors. Gradually, tents were
replaced with small trailers and, since the 1960s, Irish Travelers have
purchased large mobile homes. The size of the mobile homes has
made it difficult to pull the homes on a regular basis, causing Irish
Travelers to set up what they call camps or villages. Some of the
more affluent Georgia Travelers have been building large homes
worth over $200,000 in their villages, but this is unique to the
Georgia Travelers and the cause of much suspicion by local non-
Travelers about the source of their money. Mississippi, Georgia, and
Texas Travelers have their own villages in the South although they
remain itinerant in terms of occupations. Families will travel throughout the year for work and return periodically to their villages.

Occupational Practices

Irish Travelers began their itinerant occupations in the mid-1800s,
tinsmithing or trading horses and mules. The South had such demand
for horses and mules after the Civil War that some Travelers bought
land and built homes to provide stock for large plantations (Harper

1969, p. 13). Once settled, a few Traveler families never returned to the itinerant life-style and gradually lost membership in the ethnic group.

By the mid-1920s, some Irish Travelers began peddling linoleum and spraypainting while others continued to work with livestock. Their clients continued to be rural farmers. Travelers would spraypaint barns or sell linoleum for prices well below those of local businesses. To the farmers, Travelers provided a service they needed at a price they could afford. Most Traveler men would return to a farmer if there were any complaints and quickly correct the problems. Irish Travelers were generally well received in small towns due to their willingness to satisfy the customers (Harper 1969).

Once the use of the automobile increased in the 1930s, Travelers gave up their barrel-shaped wagons pulled by horses and replaced them with trucks. Like the wagons, the trucks carried all the Traveler family's possessions. Each night, the Travelers would set up camp near a stream or a friendly farm, using a large canvas tent with a wooden floor, or a barn was rented in a town to keep mules and horses. Renting a barn allowed a Traveler family to stay in one place for some length of time (Harper 1969, p. 13). During World War II, a number of Irish Traveler families who owned stables provided the U.S. government with mules for the war.

The Georgia legislature passed a law in 1927 that heavily taxed traveling horse traders and Gypsies (Georgia General Assembly 1927, p. 73). Many Irish Travelers were forced to change occupations. The law was to benefit the settled mule traders. Some Travelers paid the tax; others began in the linoleum business. Most Irish Travelers were spraypainting and peddling linoleum by the 1960s and continue the occupations today.

Texas Travelers primarily blacktop driveways and parking lots. A few Texas Traveler families reside with the Mississippi Travelers today, but they are the only Travelers blacktopping in the area. Various Gypsy families in the area also blacktop and repair roofs, so they must compete with these Texas Traveler families for local clients. Both groups are forced to travel long distances to get work.

Irish Travelers' horse and mule trading practices were organized with immediate family members. There were different forms of partnerships—fathers and sons, brothers, or fathers-in-law and sons-in-law.

Cousins became partners only when a more immediate family relationship was absent.

In addition to the Traveler partnership, a Black man was usually hired to help with the stock. Travelers would conduct the bargaining at farmhouses while the Black man would handle the horses or mules. The Black man would live and travel with the Irish Travelers, often learning the Cant and some of their bargaining techniques.

One informant stated that a Black man who had certain characteristics would be hired. He was usually single, willing to do manual labor, and not a threat to their business. Travelers were very protective about their trading secrets and did not want to hire a person who might "learn too much and then try to start his own business."

Irish Traveler women, historically, have not been and are not now expected to work outside the home in any capacity other than peddling. Throughout their history in the United States, the women have peddled various items, such as Irish lace and handbags. The women would receive cash, stock feed, or farm produce from the farmers for their goods. Only recently have the younger, unmarried women entered the labor force with non-Travelers. Due to their low educational level, lack of skills, and the suspicions held by non-Travelers, Irish Traveler women often must take factory jobs but are expected by the Traveler community to quit their jobs once they are married.

Traveler girls are attracted to outside jobs to provide what one Traveler called, "freedom from boredom." One 18-year-old, single Traveler woman stated:

> All we women do is go shopping and talk about having a husband and children. I'm tired of shopping, but I have to always have the newest clothes to catch a husband. At least having a job gives me something to do during the day and I have some money to buy more things.

Irish Traveler men are expected to work until their health becomes a problem. Elderly women are not expected to peddle goods but are responsible for helping to raise the grandchildren. Traveler women are responsible for all aspects of the home and the children including managing the money earned by their husbands. Most of the transactions Irish Travelers make are with cash, from paying for dinner to purchasing a new truck. Trading and bartering are still used by Travelers in business dealings. Many elderly women remain in the villages throughout the year and do not travel with their married children, as was the practice in the past. Traveler families are responsible for taking care of their elderly. Many elderly Travelers receive social security benefits but also receive additional financial support from family members. Travelers are very proud of the fact that they do not take part in the welfare system in the United States. Traveler children, from age 5, are socialized to their future roles in the community. The young girls learn to take care of younger siblings or cousins, clean the home, and manage money. The young boys begin helping their fathers in their occupations at an early age, often traveling with the older men for long periods of time.

Family Structure

Irish Traveler descent and inheritance are bilateral, although the children, as is the general custom in the United States, take the father's last name. To outsiders, Travelers appear to recognize each other as close relatives. Kinship responsibilities within the group, however, are usually limited to immediate family members and first and second cousins.

Residences are usually composed of the nuclear family. Grandparents, even when widowed, may maintain their own residences unless disabled. If his or her health is poor, a grandparent will live with a daughter and her family. The unmarried children continue to live with their parents until their marriages.

Due to the residential pattern of each group of Irish Travelers, whenever a party or ceremony involving a Traveler occurs, the entire village is invited.

ENGAGEMENT ARRANGEMENTS

Irish Travelers practice endogamy. There are more females than males within the Traveler community, so competition for marriage partners is strong.

Marriages are still arranged by the mothers, sometimes at birth, although these early agreements are often broken. A young couple may have a decision in finalizing the match, and rarely do the mothers arrange a marriage without prior approval from the couple. Traveler men are usually over 21 years of age when they marry and their brides may be as young as 12, with the average age being between 15 and 18. An exchange of money, up to $200,000 in cash for the young man, is not uncommon among the more affluent Traveler families. The less affluent Georgia Travelers have steadily increased the numbers of women who marry outside the group. Without a large dowry to offer a boy's family, these girls must choose between the possibility of remaining unmarried for life or marrying outside the group.

Mississippi, Georgia, and Texas Travelers do marry across groups, but the increasing numbers within each group contributes to a reduction in the exchange. Marriages between second cousins is acceptable to Irish Travelers and is within the law of most southern states. Local officials have adapted to the cultural practices of the Irish Travelers by expediting the needed court order from Juvenile Court for a marriage involving someone under 15.

WEDDINGS

Once the boy's parents are ready to accept an agreement with the girl's family, an announcement is made to the Traveler community— often by word of mouth. Within a day, and often hours, the couple has a marriage license and the wedding arrangements are made.

The desire for a rapid marriage ceremony once the engagement is announced is to protect the girl's family's investment. As the time increases between the engagement and the wedding, the chance for gossip about the girl's reputation also increases. In addition, the details of the dowry may slip out, allowing other Traveler mothers to offer more cash or gifts. A Traveler potential mother-in-law is often swayed by money. Georgia Travelers, due to the larger dowries, marry more quickly than Mississippi Travelers but, overall, the longest wait period is four days. Four days is enough time to order the flowers, reserve a club for the reception, contact the priest and the church, and purchase the wedding dress and tuxedos.

Multiple couples in a wedding ceremony are not uncommon. In 1985, 10 Traveler couples were married in one ceremony. These 10 couples had to go to another state to marry because the state in which they resided would not give a 12-year-old Traveler girl permission to marry. Multiple couples in a wedding are often a result of "wings." A boy's mother may agree to have her son marry a girl if the girl has a brother for her daughter. The boy is said to have a "wing"—his sister. Siblings from one family often marry siblings from another family. This type of arrangement also provides economic advantages in that partnerships are formed by the men, and the wives are more likely to become close friends. Two, however, is the most common number of couples in a wedding ceremony.

Traveler couples will usually travel together for their honeymoon trips. They state that the group trip reduces the brides' feelings of homesickness.

Traveler girls who have no brothers to whom to attach themselves for a marriage arrangement must depend upon their looks or their parents' money to arrange a spouse. Cousins may provide a "wing" if the mothers are close.

Any person with a physical disability has a poor chance of marrying due to the belief that physical disability may inhibit the man from working or the woman from having children.

Weddings are usually held after Christmas because of the likelihood of a large number of Travelers being in the villages for the holidays. The holidays provide the Travelers with a chance to arrange marriages and then to organize the ceremony before the families return to their itinerant occupations.

FUNERALS

Irish Travelers used to bury their dead once a year in a large funeral ceremony to provide a chance for other Travelers to attend. Among Georgia Travelers, the yearly burial date was April 28, while Mississippi Travelers buried their dead on May 1. Funeral homes would hold the bodies for the Travelers until the designated burial dates. Both groups of Travelers would have a Catholic church funeral with a mass and burial in a Catholic cemetery.

Today, the Travelers do not have group funerals, for a number of reasons. The costs for holding a body are high. The population of Travelers has increased so much that contact with all Travelers is limited, so attendance at funerals has decreased. There has been an increase in competition for spraypainting and blacktop customers and, as a result, Irish Traveler men travel more often, making it more difficult to take time off to return for a funeral. Returning to the South for a few months is no longer practiced by all Traveler men. Funerals are now held a few days or up to a few months after a Traveler's death. Mississippi and Georgia Travelers attend each other's funerals if they are in the South. The older children, over 10, are expected to attend funerals with their parents.

The Catholic cemeteries in which Travelers are buried are very old. Large statues and monumental stones are found at Travelers' grave sites. The statues are usually of the Infant Jesus of Prague, "the Holy Family"—Mary, Joseph, and Jesus— or Michael, "the arch-angel," or they consist of a large crucifix with Jesus. The Irish Travelers prefer to buy grave sites near the roads of the cemetery so other Travelers can see the statues and family names. Often two families may buy a number of lots and have the family names engraved on a stone with a stone bench near the plots.

Traveler funerals are very emotional services. Father Connors, the parish priest at St. Jude Church, usually performs the services for the Mississippi Travelers but other priests have been used. Traveler women usually cry and speak aloud during the service. A Traveler woman may drape herself over the coffin crying. The crying contin-ues in the cemetery. Afterward, the Travelers return to their trailer park or a rented hall for food and socializing.

There is only one funeral home in town in which the Mississippi Travelers may hold their wakes. Each night before the burial date, the Travelers hold a rosary service. A rosary service is a common practice of all Catholics but is usually limited to the night before the funeral. As the adults say the rosary, the children are unsupervised and play throughout the funeral home. As a result, the children cause some damage. Instead of trying to change their children's behaviors, Travelers prefer to pay for any damage they cause.

Although funerals are held throughout the year, they are still seen as social gatherings. In the past, Mississippi Travelers would invite the Georgia Travelers to a barbecue on the grounds of the funeral home. A hole would be dug for a pig roast for all those attending the funeral. The funeral home would allow the barbecue because the Travelers provided good business and extra money to cover what the funeral director called "headaches." The barbecue outing is no longer practiced, although a meal is usually provided to guests at a rented hall.

FIRST COMMUNIONS AND CONFIRMATIONS

Most Mississippi Traveler children do not attend Catholic schools, so church instruction on the preparation for their first communions and confirmations must be done at night or on weekends.

Catholics receive their first communion, or, as it may be called, first Eucharist, near age 8 or when the child enters second grade. The Catholic school prepares its students for first communion in religion classes during the school day and, as a class, the children take first communion during one of the Sunday masses. Travelers, however, have chosen to have their own first communion service, even if some of the children are attending the Catholic school and its preparatory classes.

Before children receive first communion, they make their first confession or reconciliation. The Catholic church believes one must be free of grave sins before receiving communion. Confession involves a meeting with the priest face-to-face or behind a partition. Catholics discuss their sins with the priest and he in turn acts as an intercessor to God for forgiveness. A penance is given to Catholics that ranges from prayers to acts of sacrifice.

Children receiving their first communion are expected to wear white outfits, symbolizing cleanliness from sin, for the service. The girls wear short white dresses with white shoes and the boys wear a white shirt, dark pants or a suit, and dark shoes.

Travelers go beyond the normative attire. Traveler girls wear long white, altered wedding gowns, with veils and trains, usually ordered out of Chicago for $200 to $400. The boys also wear white suits, white shoes, and gold necklaces with a holy medal attached. The children receiving the sacrament wear corsages or boutonnieres and their family members in the congregation wear identical flowers in smaller arrangements. A large reception is held for all the Travelers in a rented hall or the church cafeteria.

Confirmation is the Catholics' rite of passage for young adults to reconfirm their baptismal promises of faith. Catholics are usually baptized at 6 weeks old with the parents and godparents reciting the beliefs of the church for the child. At age 12, or eighth grade, the church offers the young adults the chance to accept the beliefs of the church on their own—similar to a rebaptism.

Due to the fact that many Travelers drop out of school before the eighth grade, they must take confirmation classes at night. The Travelers do not have a separate service from non-Travelers for confirmation, but, every two years, half of St. Jude's confirmation service is composed of Travelers.

For confirmation, the young adult chooses a sponsor. A sponsor is similar to the godparents for an infant. The sponsor is a person who can offer spiritual support to the young person.

At baptism, the parents give their babies Christian names. At confirmation, another name is added, although it is never used legally. The confirmation name is the name of the saint to which the person feels closest. The confirmation names are usually of the saint to whom the mother feels closest. The most common name for Traveler boys is Jude and, for girls, Anne (Mary's sister).

Irish Travelers usually choose women for their sponsors. The women are either their aunts, older sisters, or older cousins. The Traveler girls never choose men for sponsors. The Traveler boys may choose a man or a woman. If a man is chosen, he may be the boy's father, uncle, or cousin.

OTHER RELIGIOUS PRACTICES

Irish Travelers have always been Catholic and continue to raise their children in the Catholic church. Due to a lack of formal instruction, however, most Travelers have integrated some of their own religious practices into Catholic worship. Some of these practices, such as novenas or praying for a number of days for a special intention, are older Catholic practices that are now not widely encouraged by the church, due to the tendency for the followers to show signs of superstitions rather than proclamations of faith.

Traveler women are very religious, while the men participate in the sequence of sacraments but do not regularly attend church. All Travelers are baptized as infants, receive first communion around 8 years of age, and are confirmed between 12 and 18 years of age.

The women continue to attend mass and receive communion and often attend confession. The men attend mass on holidays and special events. There are some Traveler men who do attend mass weekly with their families but these are the exceptions.

Many of the older Traveler women attend mass daily. Sometimes the attendance is merely for "extra graces" but usually the women are praying for special intentions. There are four major concerns for which Travelers pray, in order of importance: that their daughters marry; that their daughters, once married, become pregnant; that their husbands or sons quit drinking; and that any health problems in the family are overcome.

Drinking is considered a problem by both Travelers and the parish priests. There are a number of admitted alcoholics among the Traveler men. The women do not drink except at weddings. The Travelers have devised what they refer to as "taking the pledge." When a Mississippi Traveler man decides to try to give up drinking, he visits the priest and together they walk over to the church. On the altar, the Traveler "pledges" out loud that he will give up drinking for a certain number of weeks or months. The priest must be there as a witness. The Traveler is then blessed by the priest and leaves the church.

The parish priest states that the Travelers are realistic in their pledges by not promising to give up alcohol for life. Pressure to "take the pledge" usually comes from the man's wife, mother, or mother-in-law. Divorce is rare among Traveler couples, but separations do occur as a result of arguments over husbands' drinking.

The methods by which Travelers pray for their special intentions are usually not limited to conventional prayers. Other than attending mass and taking the pledge, Travelers will pray to the saints and leave money in the crevices of a saint's statue in a church. St. Jude is called "the patron saint of hopeless cases" and the Travelers have made him their patron saint. Many of the male children are given the middle name Jude and, as mentioned before, some Traveler boys take the name Jude in confirmation.

Each trailer site has a yard statue of either Jesus as the Infant of Prague or a statue of Mary. An additional statue is often found in the trailer with a number of crucifixes on the walls. The purchasing of statues is still a Catholic practice, but it is currently not as widespread as in the past. Travelers extend this practice to dashboard statues in their cars, religious bumper stickers such as "Pray the Rosary," and religious necklaces and rings.

NAMING OF CHILDREN

Irish Traveler culture is matriarchal but it is neolinear in reference to the naming of the children. Travelers are known by nicknames because their legal names are often shared by many other Travelers. Among the Mississippi Travelers, for example, a Traveler father may have three brothers. All of the siblings may marry and have children. It is expected that the firstborn boy of each family will be named after the father's father. If the grandfather is named Tom Carroll, he may have four grandsons named Tom Carroll. The firstborn girl is named after the grandmother. The second child is named after the mother if a girl and the father if a boy. Later children are named after uncles, aunts, or grandparents. The Georgia Travelers have a different naming pattern. The firstborn boy is named after his father and the firstborn girl is named after her mother. Other children are named after either aunts or uncles on each side of the family (Harper 1977, p. 149). Georgia Travelers have fewer duplications of names due to their naming pattern.

To avoid confusion, nicknames are given to each, such as "Big Red" for a redheaded Traveler man and "Little Red" for his son, and these nicknames are used throughout their lives in the Traveler community. Nicknames are often used on gravestones because a

Traveler may have been known by his nickname for so long that his legal name seems unfamiliar to the family.

In school, the children usually go by their legal names. The nicknames are reserved for Traveler use as they provide protection from outsiders. If a non-Traveler visits the trailer park asking for Tom Carroll, the Travelers can honestly ask, "Which Tom Carroll?" A physical description will not help identify a Traveler because of similar characteristics. Without a Traveler's nickname, a non-Traveler is limited in the search.

PAST EDUCATIONAL EXPERIENCES

Travelers, until the 1930s, rarely attended school. Interviewing Travelers who were over 60 years old, I learned that traveling was a full-time existence, and formal education was not given a place in their lives. They learned how to read and work math from their parents to the level necessary to be successful in trading and peddling.

Harper (1977, p. 21) stated that some Travelers in the mule trading days were educated by tutors who traveled with the group, but the practice was rare and short-lived. Boarding schools in Georgia were a more common form of achieving formal education, with the boys attending a separate Catholic boarding school from the girls. The price of the boarding schools and the desire for the children to be with the parents caused only a limited number of Travelers to enroll their children in the schools. Travelers who did attend school did not go beyond the third or fourth grade.

Mississippi Travelers did not make use of boarding schools. Enrollment in Catholic schools as they traveled was the more common practice. Even with this practice, Traveler children only received a minimal level of education because of the large number of absences, transferring to other schools, and dropping out by third grade.

In the 1930s, Traveler boys began to increase their attendance in the schools, sometimes reaching high school and college. The drive for education was due to athletic ability. One Mississippi Traveler boy attended a Catholic high school for two years just to play football. Two other Mississippi Traveler boys won college football scholarships. One attended Louisiana State University and the other attended Notre Dame University. Neither returned for their second year because of low grades, but they were highly respected by the Traveler community. The respect had nothing to do with the educational achievements, however, but with the fact that the boys played football. Travelers are avid football fans and Louisiana State University and Notre Dame are their favorite teams even today because of these two Traveler boys in addition to the Catholic influence on both universities as well as the Irish orientation of Notre Dame.

SUMMARY

Irish Travelers in Ireland are salient within Irish society because of their presence in camping areas restricted to traveling peoples and their occupations, which include, but are not limited to, the collection of scrap metal, tinsmithing, and sometimes begging (in urban areas). As discussed previously, language and dress also play a part in identifying Irish Travelers. The Irish government is concerned about the welfare of Irish Travelers and this concern is often expressed through the media, which reinforces awareness of Travelers to non-Travelers.

In the United States, Irish Travelers do not suffer the same economic or social plight or media attention as Travelers in Ireland. Irish Travelers in the United States own new cars and trucks and have their own neighborhoods equal in status to any other American middle-class neighborhood. Racial and ethnic diversity in the United States is an advantage to Irish Travelers; in Ireland, diversity is not as widespread, resulting in ethnicity being more open to criticism.

Spraypainting, laying linoleum, and blacktopping are occupations shared by other Americans, but the practice of itinerancy of whole families is the cause for immediate suspicion of Irish Travelers living in the United States. Many non-Travelers do not know of the complexity of the Irish Traveler culture, only that they have an unusual life-style because of itinerancy. Those non-Travelers regularly interacting with Travelers know of the existence of the Cant as well as some of the boundary rules.

The fact that Travelers are Catholic and Irish is not the cause for prejudice or discrimination. Irish Catholic immigrants in the late 1800s and early 1900s were subjects of prejudice and discrimination, but they are now part of mainstream society even though stereotypes continue to exist (Greeley et al. 1980; Greeley 1974). Non-Travelers assume Travelers are really Gypsies, although the knowledge of Gypsy culture is based on stereotypes.

Although this chapter only briefly explains some aspects of Traveler culture, it does provide enough information to verify Travelers as a practicing ethnic group that does not share the characteristics of many Gypsy tribes. The traditions and beliefs held by Irish Travelers are significant in demonstrating that the Travelers are an accommodating rather than an acculturating group, as discussed in Chapter 2. Traveler practices have been in existence for decades, and although technology may influence their occupational practices, their desire to remain a closed community continues, still discouraging assimilation. The following chapter will present the results of the study of the educational experiences of Irish Travelers in a Catholic elementary school. Understanding some of the cultural practices that Irish Travelers display in the larger community will provide insight into understanding non-Traveler and Traveler children's perceptions and behaviors in the elementary school.

4

Gaining Access

In this research, I sought to describe the impact of Irish Traveler ethnicity in a Catholic elementary school from an ethnographic perspective. The school in which the study was conducted has been renamed St. Jude to provide anonymity. St. Jude is a Catholic elementary school located in a large southern city in the United States. The field methods of participant observation and in-depth interviews discussed by Spradley (1979, 1980) were used. From August 1986 to June 1987, I taught social studies in the junior high grades (seventh and eighth) in the morning and collected data in the classrooms in the lower grades in the afternoon. Formal and informal interviews with students, teachers, the principal, staff, and parents regularly working in the school were recorded on paper in an abbreviated form the same day and, later in the evening, were translated into long form. A file was set up with data categorized by topics.

I participated in all school activities that were expected of teachers, such as attending religious services during school hours, music and art programs, kindergarten and eighth-grade graduations, football games, and even after-school tutoring.

The enormous amount of data collected during approximately 1,260 hours provides the foundation for an in-depth analysis of Traveler children's school experiences.

This chapter will expand on the methodology by providing an in-depth discussion of the following: the development of the research topic, the setting, the students, the teachers, the theoretical background, and the research procedures.

DEVELOPMENT OF THE RESEARCH TOPIC

Gaining entry in the field is always a risky situation. Some background information is needed before explaining my specific research procedures.

During the summer of 1982, the Department of Educational Curriculum and Instruction at Texas A&M University offered a trip to England and Scotland for graduate credit, of which I took advantage. In Great Britain, I learned of a traveling group called Irish Travelers. The British government was in constant conflict with Irish Travelers by trying to move the families into settlement houses. The British people often called Irish Travelers "Gypsies." Traveling to Paris for a weekend during the trip, our group saw many French Gypsy children on the streets begging for money. I was ignorant of the fact that Gypsies still existed as an ethnic group. When I returned to Texas, I began reviewing the literature on Gypsies and found that much of the research was being conducted on different tribes or subnations of Gypsies in the United States. With a specialization in sociology, I considered studying the ethnic socialization of Rom Gypsy children in Texas (one tribe of Gypsies). After interviewing a number of researchers of Rom peoples, I was encouraged to choose another topic. Rom have very strict boundary rules, and any hopes of breaking these rules to study Rom children was not feasible within my time frame. One researcher in Texas studying Rom fortune-tellers had been in the field for a number of years before the Rom women would discuss their culture (Ruth Andersen, personal interview, 1985).

Still fascinated with Gypsy culture, I visited friends in the research area and asked about the existence of Gypsies in the city. Numerous people in retail businesses whom I knew personally discussed their experiences or knowledge of people they believed were Gypsies. Many older male Catholics interviewed reflected on past school experiences with these Gypsies in the 1940s in an all boys' Catholic high school. Although I knew the obstacles to working with Gypsies, I was still interested in these "Gypsies" that so many older locals discussed.

I learned of a trailer park in which the majority of the Gypsies resided, so I decided to drive through it. As I drove through the "bins" (the roads of the park), I saw many freckled-faced, light-skinned tenants with hair color ranging from blond to black. I immediately questioned the Gypsy label. Next to many of the trailers were four-door, American-made sedans—usually Buicks—and American-made trucks rigged for spraypainting. Many trailer sites displayed religious yard ornaments, usually of Mary, the mother of Jesus Christ, or the Infant Jesus of Prague. From the manager of the trailer park, I learned that the tenants were all Irish Travelers, earning their living as itinerant spraypainters. Half of the park was reserved for Travelers and the other for non-Travelers, separated by the main road of the park. I also was told by the trailer park manager that the Traveler children attended a Catholic elementary school nearby called St. Jude.

During the Christmas holidays in 1984, I contacted the pastor of St. Jude Church, Father Connors. Father Connors scheduled a visit with a widowed Traveler and her four daughters in the mother's trailer. Father accompanied me to the trailer to make the introductions and then left me alone with the women. The younger women, in their thirties, drove me around the "bins" and jokingly introducing me to other Traveler women as a "Georgia girl" (a Traveler from Georgia). I explained to the Traveler women that I wanted to write my dissertation on their group, which they took to mean a book. After a couple of hours with the Traveler women in the car, I knew I had come upon a unique cultural enclave that had strong boundary rules but that would not be as difficult to study as Rom. The Travelers did not understand the extent of my task, however, for one woman at the end of our meeting said, "I hope you have enough to write your book." During 1985, I maintained contact with Father Connors while at Texas A&M, always planning to return to the city to conduct my dissertation research on Irish Travelers.

I had hoped to compare the Travelers' school experience at St. Jude with that of the one public school in which 90 Travelers were enrolled. Gaining access to public school classrooms in the research area is a major endeavor, and the research department at the central office for the public schools could not guarantee approval for the topic. The more I read of ethnographic methodology and Traveler customs, the more I questioned the task of studying two schools. I already had the approval of the pastor of St. Jude, Father Connors; the principal, Sister Catherine; and Sister Anne of the diocesan school office. I decided to limit my dissertation research to St. Jude School, interviewing children randomly in the school with classroom observations three times a week while working at a different site part-time.

I again changed my plan for St. Jude by accepting a part-time position as the seventh- and eighth-grade social studies teacher. In this capacity, I was able to collect in-depth data from Travelers and non-Travelers in the school. Students and teachers viewed me as a legitimate member of the school environment. Instead of a non-participant observer, I became a participant observer, keeping in perspective my potential biases as a teacher.

THE SETTING

The Student Population

In the 1960s, the research area began to experience integration. By 1986, the Black population in the area had gradually increased, with Whites moving to the newer sections of the city.

St. Jude has been affected by the racial changes in the area. During the past 10 years, enrollment at St. Jude has decreased from 689 to 384 students in grades one to eight. The change in the area's racial composition has left a much smaller number of Catholics in the parish, due to the fact that the Catholic church in the city is predominantly White. Most of the Catholics remaining in the parish are older couples who cannot afford to move. Although, nationwide, fewer Catholic parents are sending their children to Catholic elementary schools, the percentage attending Catholic schools in this city is still higher than the national average. All Catholic schools in the city are not experiencing similar enrollment patterns, however. While the Catholic schools in the newer sections of the city have long waiting lists for student enrollment, the inner-city Catholic schools are suffering financially because the neighborhoods are no longer composed of Catholic families. Catholics in the newer sections of the city are not choosing to enroll their children in the inner-city Catholic schools, so the diocesan office has had to close a number of inner-city schools only to plan to build new ones in the suburbs.

Many of the Catholics enrolled in St. Jude are parishioners of other Catholic churches, not from this city but from nearby cities. There is only one Catholic school in the bordering county, and St. Jude is closer than their county's school for many families.

There are some Black Catholic families in St. Jude parish, but Blacks in the South have not traditionally been Catholic, and their numbers do not replace the number of White Catholics moving out of the parish. Blacks constitute 10% of the St. Jude School population (kindergarten to grade eight) and non-Catholics constitute 20% (many of the Blacks are included in the non-Catholic count).

The following gives a breakdown of the White non-Travelers, Travelers, and Blacks at St. Jude School during the 1986-87 school year, grades kindergarten through eight: for non-Travelers, 77.6% were White (N = 337) and 9.9% were Black (N = 43); Travelers constituted 12.4% of this population (N = 54).

An increasing number of middle-class Blacks in the city are being seen in large numbers in private schools, particularly Catholic schools. The Blacks attending St. Jude are predominantly middle class and choose St. Jude over the public schools in the area because they believe St. Jude provides a safe academic environment for their children.

Irish Travelers are the third type of group enrolled in large numbers at St. Jude. The Irish Travelers reside in a trailer park within St. Jude parish. There are 240 trailer sites rented by Travelers, although the number of Travelers residing in the park is unknown. The resident manager estimates between 900 and 1,000 individuals.

The Diocese keeps statistics on the racial composition of each Catholic elementary school within the Diocese but classifies Irish Travelers as White. At St. Jude, the identity of the Travelers is noted

Table 4.1 Traveler/Non-Traveler Student Population by Sex and Grade Level: St. Jude School 1986-87

Grade Level	Travelers Males	Females	Total Travelers	Non-Travelers Males	Females	Total Non-Trav.	Total All
Kindergarten	8	6	14 (28.0%)	16	20	36 (72.0%)	50
First grade	5	5	10 (18.9%)	26	17	43 (81.1%)	53
Second grade	4	1	5 (9.8%)	28	18	46 (90.2%)	51
Third grade	3	4	7 (14.6%)	13	28	41 (85.4%)	48
Fourth grade	5	3	8 (16.3%)	22	19	41 (83.7%)	49
Fifth grade[a]	1	0	1 (4.5%)	9	12	21 (95.5%)	22
Sixth grade	0	2	2 (4.4%)	16	27	43 (95.6%)	45
Seventh grade	5	1	6 (12.0%)	26	18	44 (88.0%)	50
Eighth grade[a]	1	0	1 (4.2%)	6	17	23 (95.8%)	24

a. In fifth and eighth grades, only the homeroom in which the Traveler student was enrolled was counted in the table. Counting all homerooms, however, the total school population at St. Jude for the school year 1986-87 was 434, with 12.4% being Irish Travelers and 87.6% being non-Travelers.

by the secretary to ease the transition of late-coming Traveler children into the school. Table 4.1 shows the Traveler/non-Traveler breakdown for the 1986-87 school year by grade and sex.

The Teachers

For the year of the study, St. Jude had 16 classroom teachers with a mean age of 38 and 7.8 years of teaching experience. A number of the teachers had been at St. Jude for their total teaching careers.

During the 1986-87 school year, there were seven classroom teachers new to the school, of which I was one, with only one junior high teacher teaching for the first time. The biggest turnover of teachers from the previous year was found in the junior high, with five out of six teachers new to St. Jude.

Many of the young teachers were from out of state and had moved to the city so their husbands could attend a college in the area. For various reasons, such as fear of the conditions in the public schools or discouragement by the competition to obtain a position with the city school system, the young teachers chose the diocesan school system in which to teach. Only two teachers, both new, were non-Catholic.

The principal, Sister Catherine, had been appointed to St. Jude in August 1986. Sister had transferred from a university setting to accept the position of elementary school principal of St. Jude. Being from a traditional religious order, as were the other two sisters teaching in the school, Sister Catherine believed in strict discipline and obedience in the school although no corporal punishment or "meaningless punishments" were allowed, such as copying information from books or standing in a corner.

PROCEDURES

Theoretical Background

The philosophical base for the proposed study is phenomenology, or the view that humans act on how they interpret their world; reality is defined by humans. To understand Irish Travelers in the elementary school, in my research, I attempted to identify their interpretations through Weber's concept of *verstehen,* or the "emphatic understanding or an ability to reproduce in one's mind the feelings, motives, and thoughts behind the actions of others" (Bogdan and Taylor 1975, p. 14). The phenomenologist attempts to describe a social setting from the point of view of the observed.

Symbolic interaction provides the theoretical framework for the phenomenologist with the major works from John Dewey ([1938] 1968), Charles H. Cooley ([1902] 1964), Robert Park ([1925] 1967), W. I. Thomas ([1931] 1966), and George Herbert Mead ([1934] 1966). Symbolic interaction has three basic assumptions: (a) Social reality is a social production; (b) humans are capable of shaping and guiding their own behavior; and (c) while shaping and guiding their behaviors, they interact with others. "The interactionist assumes that humans learn their basic symbols, their conceptions of self, and the definitions they attach to social objects through interaction with others." Human interaction is the basic source of data (Denzin 1978, p. 7).

Naturalistic inquiry provides the methodological inquiry mode for symbolic interaction theory. According to Wolf and Tymitz (1977,

p. 7), naturalistic inquiry attempts to capture, "actualities, social realities, and human perceptions that exist untainted by the obtrusiveness of formal measurement of preconceived questions." Naturalistic inquiry shares the basic assumptions and objectives of verstehen and symbolic interaction (Denzin 1978, p. 78).

Research Methodology

Unfortunately, no single methodology adequately considers all causal factors (Denzin 1978, p. 28) or meets the requirements of symbolic interaction theory: "Because each method reveals different aspects of empirical reality, multiple methods of observations must be employed. This is termed triangulation" (Denzin 1978, p. 28). In this research study, triangulation was practiced through the use of observations over time, in-depth interviewing, sociometric tests, and collection of data from school records.

The foundation for ethnography, as emphasized in the theory of symbolic interaction, is collecting data on the natives' point of view—that is, on those in the school environment. *Ethnography* is defined as

> the work describing a culture. The essential core of this activity aims to understand another way of life from the native point of view. Rather than studying people, ethnography means learning from people. (Spradley 1979, p. 3)

Learning from people requires an openness of mind that is not found in the traditional scientific process. The scientific inquiry process involves selecting a problem, formulating hypotheses, collecting and analyzing data, and, finally, drawing conclusions. Ethnographic research does not require a preconceived hypothesis because, in the process of ethnography, one may not assume the research participants' feelings or perceptions of a social situation before entering the field.

Using Geertz's (1973) methodology of "thick description," and Glazer and Strauss's Grounded Theory approach (1967), I analyzed field notes throughout the study. By comparing one day's observations with the notes taken the week before, salient themes of action were identified. Modification of data collection was constant throughout the school year to fill in gaps. The researcher may not expect to be absent of personal biases, but an awareness of these biases is the first step in their control.

Using ethnography, the researcher must make the familiar strange and the strange familiar so that biases are reduced and the natives' interpretations are recorded. The elementary school is a difficult site to view as a strange place because most of us have been participants. In addition, being previously employed as an elementary teacher, I had to work even harder in my research so as not to view the entire school setting only through the eyes of a teacher.

One methodology within the field of ethnography is participant observation. As a participant observer, a researcher enters the field as a participant, still being an objective observer. I took a teaching position for seventh- and eighth-grade social studies. Ethnographic studies in which the researcher has been a participant observer have been very successful, for example: *Tally's Corner* (Liebow 1967), *The Cocktail Waitress* (Spradley and Mann 1975), *Black Like Me* (Griffin 1962), *"Shut Those Thick Lips!"* (Rosenfeld 1971), and *Asylums* (Goffman 1961).

For the research study, there were no coding systems or questionnaires used other than a sociometric test. Unstructured interviewing techniques were used because there is concern about

> which questions are appropriate to ask, how they should be worded so as to be nonthreatening or unambiguous, which questions to include or exclude to best learn about the topic under study, or what constitutes an answer. Appropriate or relevant questions are seen to emerge from the process of interaction that occurs between the interviewer and interviewee. (Schwartz and Jacobs 1979, p. 40)

Coding systems are also limiting. There are more than 100 coding systems designed to observe, describe, and analyze aspects of classroom interaction, such as those found in Amidon and Flanders (1963), Anderson (1939), Cogan (1956), Sinclair and Coulthard (1975), and Withall (1949). "How can interaction be viewed as a unidirectional exchange in which teachers talk and students respond, or vice-versa? The critical issue of the how, or the underlying processes, appears to have faded amidst these literally thousands of mostly quantitative, cross-sectional studies" (Denton 1983, pp. 2-3).

Although a preconceived coding system was not used in the research, a sociometric test, first devised by Moreno (1934), was used to help analyze the social structure of the classroom. Sociometry is "a method of evaluating the feelings of the group members toward each other with respect to a common criterion" and "the most extensive use of the sociometric test has been in school settings" (Gronlund 1959, p. 3). Gronlund (1959, p. 2) explains the use of sociometry in school settings, stating, "Teachers and research workers alike have used this technique to study the extent to which individual pupils were accepted by their peers and to analyze the social structure of classroom groups."

At St. Jude, the students were asked only about two dimensions of school interaction: work and play—choices for playmates and choices for a class project. The questions were presented to each classroom twice, in December and in April. Observations and informal interviewing throughout the year helped to verify students' choices on the sociometric test. Sociometric tests have been analyzed and found to be valid (see Byrd 1946, p. 21). The specific methodological procedures used in the research study will be discussed later in this chapter.

Initial Explanations in the Field

In summer 1986, a new principal, Sister Catherine, was appointed to St. Jude School. Sister knew little of my research but had dealt with Irish Travelers as a teacher at St. Jude years before. Father Connors assured Sister Catherine that my research would be to the school's benefit. Sister Catherine asked only one thing—that I not tell the teachers of my specific research topic. This idea better suited the research objective. If the teachers knew, it would bias their conversations with and around me as well as their behaviors. At the first faculty meeting, Sister Catherine introduced all the new teachers, of which I was one, and told everyone I would be observing their classrooms throughout the year, collecting research on children's interaction patterns. The teachers seemed suspicious at first, but, once the children returned to school, I was the least of their concerns.

Observations and Interviews

For three months, every afternoon of the fall semester in 1986, I observed in one or more classrooms, the lunchroom, library classes, computer classes, hallways, physical education classes, and the recess grounds.

I found a social division between the teachers in the primary grades (K-2), middle grades (3-5), and junior high grades (6-8). Teachers, due to schedules and classroom activities, would often socialize within their groups. Being a junior high teacher and observing a second-grade classroom, for example, did not always bring instant rapport with the teacher or her students. Many younger students never saw me on campus except during the time I was observing their class, because the junior high classrooms are in a different building than that for the lower grades. I also found that younger children are somewhat afraid of the upper grade teachers because they have heard stories about how "tough" they are on their students.

In November 1986, I realized I needed to develop better rapport with the teachers and students in the lower grades so I volunteered to teach map skills to each classroom in the afternoons. This provided a legitimate reason for my presence in the classroom, and it allowed me to improve my rapport with the teachers and the students. I spent 30 minutes with each class once a week but continued my observations throughout the school. The decision to teach in the lower grades brought instant success. Although I had much more preparation and grading to do, the teachers appreciated the 30 minutes off, and both the teachers and the students were more willing to engage in conversation outside the classroom. Traveler children, especially, would talk to me during their entire recess period because I was now one of their teachers. Although the 30 minutes a week I taught in each classroom was a time during which I was unable to observe the regular classroom teacher, I still collected an enormous amount of information.

In addition to unstructured interviewing and observations, I chose to use a sociometric test in December and in April with all of the children at St. Jude, following the design of Caldwell (1959, pp. 12-13). For each of the classrooms, except kindergarten, I asked the students to write on a piece of paper three people they like playing with at recess. On the board, I wrote the word *play* and listed the numbers 1, 2, and 3. The students were to copy my format on their papers. I explained that the choices were to be from their homeroom and the numbers corresponded with their first choice through their third choice. I allowed the students to ask questions if they did not understand my directions. Some students did not give a third choice. I limited the choices to homerooms rather than grade levels because the teachers often brought the children outside as a class and not as a grade level. Also, observing interaction in the classroom would be limited only to the classroom students, so I wanted the sociometric tests to be consistent. After the students wrote their choices for play, I asked them to write the word *work* on their paper with the numbers 1, 2, and 3 under the word. I explained that I wanted them to choose 3 people from their room with whom they would like to work if the teacher wanted a poster made or a project completed. I emphasized that they should choose three people who would help them do a good job. I again explained that number 1 meant their first choice and so on, as before. I collected the papers and explained that I might use some of them for projects I would have in my map skills class with them and that their teacher would also be able to group them better for work.

For kindergartners, I asked each child to give me his or her choices and I wrote the choices on my paper. During an art activity, I asked each child, individually, to come to a corner of the room. I asked each child for the choices, as described for the older students. If they could not give me a name of a student, I asked them to point to the student in the room.

CHOSEN

CHOOSER	Amy	Ginny	Mark	Anna	Winnie	Kim	Brooke	Maureen	Henry	Della	Maria	Angelina	Elizabeth	Tommy	Joanne	Jason	Janessa	Alicia	Evan
Amy		A					B											C	
Ginny	A										B								
Mark										C									B
Anna							A		A		B					C		C	
Winnie				A					Ax		C							B	
Kim	A			B				C	Bx										
Brooke								C				B						A	
Maureen												C					B	A	
Henry	B																		A
Delia											C						B	A	
Maria									Ax	C								B	
Angelina								A									C		
Elizabeth									Ax		C							B	
Tommy											Cx						Bx	Ax	
Joanne	C						B		B									A	
Jason			C									B							
Janessa						A													
Alicia												C					B		A
Evan								A	A							C			
1st - As	2	1	0	1	0	1	1	2	5	0	0	0	0	0	0	0	0	5	2
2nd - Bs	1	0	0	1	0	0	2	0	2	0	2	2	0	0	0	0	4	3	1
3rd - Cs	1	0	1	0	0	0	0	2	0	2	4	2	0	0	0	2	1	2	0
TOTAL A=3 B=2 C=1	9	3	1	5	0	3	7	8	19	2	8	6	0	0	0	2	9	23	8

TOTAL CHOICES 113   Mutual 9   Intersex 7   Stars 2   Isolates 4

Figure 4.1. Sociometric Matrix: Work Dimension

53

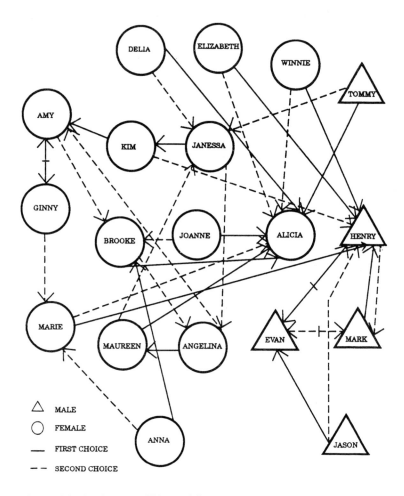

Figure 4.2. Sociogram of Figure 4.1

I repeated the same procedures for all the grade levels in April. My observations of interactions and my interviews helped provide insight into the reality and interpretations of the sociometric test.

There are three important considerations that one must take into account when administering sociometric tests: (a) Make the situations real for the students before asking them to make choices. This will help the students make choices that are close to actual behavior or actual desires. (b) Ensure the students that their choices will only be seen by the teacher and the researcher (or other teacher); their choices are to be held in secret. (c) Provide a written list of names of students, on the board or on a chart. This will decrease the students' concerns about misspelling, looking around the room at other students, or forgetting to consider an absent student.

Once the questions were answered, the results were placed in a matrix as in Figure 4.1. The students' names were written across the top and the left side of the chart. The choice number was changed to A for first choice, B for second choice, and C for third choice. The matrix was completed using these three letters.

Italicized letters represent a mutual choice. A small "x" next to a letter represents a student of one sex choosing a student of the opposite sex (called "intersex"). Once all the letters were placed in the matrix, the tabulations were made to complete each column (see Figure 4.1).

The terms *stars* and *isolates* are used in the tabulations. A "star" is a person who receives a large number of choices—a popular child for the particular criterion. An "isolate" is an individual who receives no choices on a sociometric test.

From the matrix, the data were converted into a sociogram. A sociogram is a graphic representation of the sociometric structure of a group "with the members being represented by small circles or triangles and choices represented by lines drawn between the figures" (Gronlund 1959, p. 3). Figure 4.2 shows an example of a sociogram using the data from Figure 4.1. Only one classroom sociogram has been included in this manuscript. Although matrixes and sociograms were constructed for each classroom containing Irish Travelers, they were not included in the manuscript to ensure anonymity for the students.

Trustworthiness of the Study

Guba (1981) uses the term *trustworthiness* in discussing the verification of the research findings. Verification requires assessing validity, reliability, and objectivity.

In this study, validity and generalizability were ensured through a prolonged period at the school (10 months); multiple observations over time; peer debriefing (discussing findings with teachers and university committee members); triangulation (e.g., cross-checking interpretations with teachers and students); collection of referential adequacy materials (e.g., grade reports, attendance records, observation, and interview notes); and thick descriptive data. Reliability and objectivity were ensured through overlap methods (e.g., sociograms); member checks (e.g., asking participants the same question at another time and asking other participants the same question to verify the first informant's answer); and thick descriptions.

5

School Experiences

The results of the study are presented in this chapter. The grade levels have been divided into five groups. Kindergarten is discussed by itself because of the large number of Irish Traveler students and the difference in the curriculum from the first grade. The other grades will be grouped separately as follows: first and second grades, third and fourth grades, fifth and sixth grades, and seventh and eighth grades. These grades were grouped in this way because of the natural division within the school that includes similar curricula and shared recess and lunch schedules.

There are five different relationships that emerged from the data in reference to the school setting: parents and teachers, teachers and students, non-Traveler students and Traveler students, Traveler students and other Traveler students, and, finally, Traveler students and the overall school environment. Each relationship is discussed for the five groups.

GENERAL INFORMATION

St. Jude School begins classes at the end of August and concludes at the beginning of June. The Catholic school system follows the state's rule that children absent for more than 30 days of school can be retained.

The Irish Traveler students return to school at various times throughout the fall semester, and most Traveler children are in school by the middle of November. St. Jude requires Irish Travelers to preregister their children and prepay the tuition for September to reserve a place for them. Although a Traveler child may not be in the classroom until November, the mother typically pays the tuition for the month of September and often for October during the early part of the summer. St. Jude requests verification of school attendance for Traveler children for days missed in September and October. The verification allows St. Jude to include the early school year attendance with the remaining school year to avoid retention of Traveler children based only on attendance at St. Jude.

When the Travelers return to school, they are placed in a classroom. The teachers may have a list of Traveler students on the roll but it is not a permanent one. The principal and the secretary are conscious of the distribution of Traveler children among classrooms. The general rule is to evenly distribute Travelers, even if one Traveler is separated from the only other Traveler. This separation is done to discourage Traveler children's "clannish" behavior and to allow the teacher to provide more individualized "catch-up" instruction to the student before another Traveler enrolls with additional needs. The separation is only temporary in most grade levels because a third and fourth Traveler may enroll within days of the first and second.

Traveler mothers often request that their children be separated from other Travelers in the classroom. The school's practice of separating Travelers, however, occurs without consent from the Traveler mothers. Separation from another Traveler may be requested because of conflicts in the trailer park between families. If two Traveler students are best friends, one Traveler mother may request their separation to encourage better concentration on schoolwork.

Traveler mothers often request a specific teacher for their children. Two reasons for this request are that (a) the requested teacher gives less homework or (b) the requested teacher is less structured in her teaching style.

Usually these requests are met, although the Traveler mother does not reveal these reasons to the principal. Instead, the Traveler mother may compliment the preferred teacher and tell the principal how much better her child would perform if placed in the teacher's classroom.

To avoid having the missed school days count as absences, Travelers must provide proof that their children have been enrolled in a school in the area in which they traveled. Most Travelers do provide this verification or provide the name and address of the school they attended. The secretary follows up on requesting verification from the school but sometimes the information is never received, and obtaining this verification is not a priority of St. Jude.

If a Traveler child is preregistered at St. Jude but fails to enroll, the secretary often asks other Traveler women who visit the school office about the child. The women always say the child is attending the public school. The secretary, however, does not verify this information with the public school. Parents are difficult to reach by telephone because most Travelers disconnect their telephones before they leave for the summer and often do not reconnect telephone services under the same name. The preregistration form may not have a phone number, it may have an old number, or it may have a temporary number for the summer.

As the Travelers begin planning for the summer itinerant work, the children are taken out of school. To avoid missed days counting as absences, the school has the parents officially withdraw their children from school. The parents are supposed to enroll their children in other schools in the area in which they travel for the remainder of the school year but St. Jude has no way to enforce this rule. The teacher-assigned academic grades for the shortened school year are used to determine whether a child will pass to the next grade or be retained. Once a Traveler family knows the status of their child's grade level for the next year, additional school days in another school are meaningless. Table 5.1 shows the mean for absences of Travelers and non-Travelers by sex and grade level.

KINDERGARTEN

As noted in Table 4.1, there were 50 children in kindergarten during the school year in which the data were collected, with 25 in Mrs. KA's class and 25 in Mrs. KB's class. Out of these children, 14 were Irish Travelers (6 females and 8 males). One Traveler was preregistered but did not show up for school. Irish Travelers composed 28% of the kindergarten class, the highest percentage of any grade level.

Table 5.1 Average Number of Absences for Travelers/Non-Travelers by Sex and Grade Level: St. Jude School 1986-87

| Grade Level | Travelers | | Total Travelers | Non-Travelers | | Total Non-Trav. |
	Males	Females		Males	Females	
Kindergarten	4.87	7.0	5.79	5.06	4.70	4.86
range	(1-14)	(1-12)		(0-13)	(0-15)	
First grade	4.8	5.4	5.1	6.1	6.38	6.21
	(1-11)	(2-15)		(0-13)	(0-13)	
Second grade	14.88	13.0	14.5	6.04	9.39	7.35
	(8-23.5)	(13)		(0-24.5)	(3-20)	
Third grade	8.33	6.0	7.0	6.97	6.21	6.43
	(7-9)	(4-7)		(1-21)	(0-16)	
Fourth grade	14.5	9.0	12.44	5.48	4.95	5.23
	(6-29)	(4-15)		(0-15)	(0-10)	
Fifth grade	25.5	—	25.5	4.67	8.13	6.64
	(25.5)			(0-9.5)	(0-24)	
Sixth grade	—	10.0	10.0	4.5	7.11	6.14
		(10)		(0-12)	(0-25)	
Seventh grade	8.8	18.0	10.33	4.85	5.75	5.22
	(6-14)	(18)		(0-21)	(0-12)	
Eighth grade	0	—	0	8.83	8.18	8.35
	(0)			(1-23)	(0-27)	

The two kindergarten teachers are in their early twenties with a few years of teaching experience at St. Jude. Through these years, they have developed a wide range of knowledge of Irish Traveler culture.

Most of the Irish Traveler kindergartners enter St. Jude between the last week of October and the first week of November. Many of the children had not been enrolled in kindergartens elsewhere because the Traveler mothers felt the adjustment would be too difficult. The teachers strongly suggested tutoring sessions so the children would catch up with the rest of the children. The kindergarten teachers did not follow the schedule suggested for kindergarten by the diocesan office with the non-Traveler children in the first two months of school because the teachers believed the Traveler students would be too far behind when they entered school in October and November. Once the Travelers enrolled, the pace of instruction increased. All the Traveler mothers agreed to have their kindergartners tutored after school for three or four days a week for approximately one hour per session. Tutoring continued throughout the school year with a reduction in number of sessions.

Kindergartners participated in a graduation ceremony that was required of all the students. No Traveler child withdrew from school before graduation. Graduation occurred two weeks before the rest of the school was dismissed, so many Traveler parents did not complain about graduation attendance—they often had other children in the upper grades and withdrawing these older children from school early also caused friction with the principal. As a result, Traveler mothers rarely made the attempt to withdraw their children early.

Teachers and Parents

Parents and teachers of kindergarten children often communicate with each other more than at any other grade level. For many children, kindergarten is the first school experience. Although some of the children had attended preschool, kindergarten is often viewed as the beginning of the academic years. Preschool is not always seen as an academic experience but as an alternative to day care. Traveler mothers do not enroll their children in preschool because they usually do not work outside the home. They tend to be very protective of their children, especially when non-Travelers are involved. Traveler mothers also view kindergarten as the beginning of the child's academic years but realize their children's academic years will be much shorter than those of most non-Traveler children.

Every afternoon, one will see at least one Traveler mother discussing her child's progress with a kindergarten teacher. Traveler mothers have a very positive attitude toward their children's kindergarten education. Due to the constant communication between parent and teacher, the Traveler women tend to discuss their aspirations for their children and their Traveler culture. Even grandmothers get involved in the children's education by talking with the teachers.

Traveler mothers pay the teacher for tutoring at the end of the day. The tutoring charge of $10 per hour was approved by the principal. The Traveler mother comes to the classroom to pay the teacher. This practice increases the communication between Traveler mothers and teachers concerning the students.

All of the Traveler women I interviewed as well as the kindergarten teachers expressed a hope that their children would graduate from eighth grade—especially the boys. They want their children to learn to read and master mathematics to increase their chances for work outside of painting but not outside of itinerant work. The parents never said they would like to see their children move out of the Traveler community. The mothers in the study were in their early twenties and were strongly attached to Irish Traveler culture. Their group membership is even more important to them because they will teach Traveler norms and values to their children.

The elderly grandmothers are able to step back and critique the Travelers because they no longer play a significant part in the socialization of the grandchildren. For instance, one Traveler grandmother often visited with one of the kindergarten teachers in her classroom. Once the teacher believed she had developed a friendship with the elderly Traveler, she tried to make plans to visit her in the Traveler trailer park. The Traveler, however, quickly reminded the teacher of the group's boundary rules. One elderly woman said: "Oh, no! You can't come to my trailer! Everyone will know you are there and they will drag me! We aren't suppos' to make friends with country people. If we do we will get dragged. I can meet you at a restaurant but don't come to my trailer!" Being "dragged" refers to the spreading of gossip throughout the Traveler community, which can result in being excluded from group activities such as parties. If dragging becomes fierce, one's family's reputation may be marked. Dragging or the threat of dragging becomes a significant form of social control.

The teacher had erroneously assumed that elderly Travelers could "bend the rules" more easily than younger Travelers. Although it is a matriarchal society, the Traveler women are also restricted by their own rules.

Teachers and Students

Both teachers have assigned seating for the students but frequently move children to increase socialization skills. The teachers try to separate the Travelers as much as possible because of their constant talking in the classroom. Two Travelers are often found at one table, however, because there are so many Traveler children in both kindergarten classrooms. Although the Travelers do not present discipline problems for the teachers, they do talk to each other during instructional periods if they are sitting close together.

The teachers are fairly strict in their discipline procedures. Positive reinforcement is predominantly used although a mild reprimand is often seen as necessary for out-of-the-ordinary misbehavior. No corporal punishment is used. The child misbehaving must offer an apology and a hug to the child offended.

School Interactions

To uncover group structure, I used a sociometric test (Moreno 1934). I interviewed the kindergarten children individually in December 1986 and again in April 1987, asking them to tell me three people they like playing with and three people they would like to work with on a poster for their teacher. I kept each child in the classroom so he or she could see the rest of the students when choosing. With this information, I compiled matrixes and sociograms and noted changes. I also observed and interviewed kindergartners in other school settings, such as during recess, lunch, and physical education class, and in hallways and rest rooms throughout the school year.

Early Interactions

In the first sociometric test, all but one of the Traveler children chose other Travelers as first and usually as second choices in the work and play situations, or "dimensions." When asked why they chose a particular person, Traveler children typically answered, "Because she [or he] is my cousin." Any non-Traveler chosen by a Traveler was a child whom other non-Travelers chose—a popular child. One Black child, in particular, was a common choice among Travelers and non-Travelers.

Traveler children were rarely chosen by non-Travelers. One non-Traveler did, however, choose a Traveler as first in the work dimension and two Travelers as second and third choices in the play dimension. The non-Traveler who chose the Travelers, however, was an isolate—he or she was never chosen for first, second, or third by any kindergartner.

In the classroom, Traveler children interacted well with non-Traveler children, but, if the teacher allowed the children to choose their own seats for an art activity, Traveler girls quickly sat together. Traveler boys often stayed in their regular seats, but any need for the sharing of supplies was met with other Travelers rather than with non-Travelers.

On the playground, Traveler boys and girls played in one group, occasionally allowing a single non-Traveler to join their game. When I asked non-Travelers why the children always played together (not using the term *Traveler*), they easily explained the family relationships. Playing with one's cousins was readily acceptable behavior by kindergartners, both Travelers and non-Travelers, because kindergarten was a new setting for all the children. The children believed a familiar classmate such as a cousin made the adjustment much easier.

Out of 47 kindergartners, only 1 Traveler girl and 1 non-Traveler girl had heard one of the terms *Traveler, Irish Traveler,* or *Gypsy.* When asked if she knew what an *Irish Traveler* was, a Traveler said, "That's what I am." I asked, "What does that mean?" She replied, "I don't know." She had never heard the term *Gypsy.* One non-Traveler girl had heard the term *Gypsy* but did not know what it meant.

Later Interactions

By April, the children displayed an increase in confidence in their schoolwork and social place in the classroom. Using the same method of interviewing the children individually, it was established that the explanations for choices had changed.

Travelers continued to choose other Travelers in the work and play dimensions and never chose a non-Traveler. There were no Travelers chosen by non-Travelers. Even the isolate chose non-Travelers by April. When asked why Travelers played alone (not using the term

Travelers), the non-Travelers gave up the explanation of family relationships. Instead, the children said, "Because they won't let anybody else play with them" or "Because they are mean." The children accepted the Travelers' playing with their cousins at the beginning of the year because they were new to the school but, by the end of the school year, the children were expecting to make new friends. Travelers continued to emphasize the family relationships they held with each other, but never used the terms *Traveler* or *Irish Traveler*.

Although non-Travelers viewed Traveler children as snobs on the playground, no confrontation ever occurred to change the play groups. Traveler children were unaware that non-Travelers looked down upon their restricting their play to relatives. The norms, or expected behaviors, for one group were not the norms for the other group.

Absences

There was a significant difference in the number of absences for Travelers between the two different classrooms. The average number of absences for all the students in one classroom was 7.52 (range = 0-20). The average number of days missed by Travelers from this same classroom was 9.7, with one child missing 20 days (range = 4-20). In the other classroom, the overall average was 3.52 days missed (range = 0-12), with Travelers missing an average of 3.71 days (range = 1-8). Although it is difficult to identify the cause of the difference, the teachers both agree that one was more structured than the other and provided more whole-group instruction rather than individualized instruction. The more structured teacher had the higher absentee rates among Travelers. Non-Travelers' absences were similar between classrooms.

Kindergarten Graduation

St. Jude has a kindergarten graduation ceremony every year, two weeks before the end of the school year. The children practice songs and poems for weeks to perform in front of their parents and friends at the graduation ceremony. Once the ceremony is over, the kindergartners do not return to school, beginning their summer vacation two weeks before the rest of the school.

Every kindergartner attended the 1987 graduation. The assembly was the largest gathering of Irish Traveler families of any held by the school.

Traveler children could instantly be seen in line due to their unusual clothing. The girls wore expensive dresses of gold or lace with hundreds of sequins and beads. Sequins and beads were also found on the girls' shoes and on their hair barrettes and ribbons. Traveler girls also wore gold-looped earrings and gold, add-a-bead necklaces. Traveler boys wore three-piece suits with a religious medal on a heavy gold necklace, worn outside the shirt.

Non-Traveler children constantly stared at the Travelers' outfits while waiting in line to enter the auditorium, but they didn't comment. The stares were not ones of disapproval but of curiosity to see someone their age so dressed up and so "adultlike."

Traveler parents filled up the front part of the auditorium. They all sat together, taking pictures with video cameras and 35-mm cameras of any Traveler child reciting a poem or receiving a diploma. Traveler children were well represented in the ceremony but not favored above non-Travelers.

Once the ceremony was completed, refreshments were served and families quickly took hold of their kindergartners. The children did not interact with any other kindergartners once in their families' grasp. A few non-Traveler parents introduced themselves to other non-Traveler parents but the Traveler families were not approached. Traveler families stayed to themselves with no salient interest in conversing with non-Traveler parents. All the kindergartners seemed to be pulled around by family members and, due to their age rather than any negative feelings toward one another, did not interact.

Summary of Kindergarten

The two kindergarten teachers did not demonstrate any significant differences in how they interacted with Traveler children versus non-Traveler children in school-related experiences. The tutoring of Travelers was seen as a catch-up period rather than being due to a lack of ability on the part of the children. Non-Travelers were also tutored sporadically and joined Travelers in an afternoon session if the same skills were needed. Many Traveler mothers wanted to continue the tutoring sessions even after their children had mastered the concept or skill in hopes of their children knowing more than others. A fee was charged and many teachers believed Travelers viewed tutoring as a status symbol. One teacher said, "Travelers believe that if a Traveler family can pay for private education and after-school tutoring, they must be doing very well." Traveler mothers explained the competitive emphasis within their culture as a negative force but one in which everyone must take part to be accepted. Spending money on anything, even tutoring, is an excellent way to show your family's economic status, which contributes to the family's social status.

The changes in behaviors and attitudes were primarily among the non-Traveler children. Traveler children socialized with other Travelers throughout the school year, and any awareness of Irish Traveler ethnicity was not demonstrated. Even Cant, the Travelers' secret language, was never heard by myself or the kindergarten teachers. Among the non-Travelers, however, the interpretation of the close-knit relationship of Travelers changed over time. A group of Travelers seen as playing together during recess because they were relatives were later perceived by non-Traveler children as a group of snobs. Travelers, even in kindergarten, encouraged non-Traveler children to be aware of differences, because, even though they may not have played an active role in this perception, they did not encourage more interaction and group games at recess, which might have reduced cliques.

Kindergartners would often openly discuss home life. For example, Traveler children would discuss where they had eaten dinner the night before. Anytime a restaurant was mentioned, a Traveler would say he or she had eaten there. I asked jokingly, "Do you go out to eat every night?" The child said, "Yes. My mother only fixes breakfast. On Saturday and Sunday we go out for lunch and dinner." I later found that eating out was a common practice among Travelers. At the beginning of the year, an unusual practice such as this was discussed by the kindergarten Travelers naively—not aware that

other families eat at home more often. As the year progressed, with
questioning of this and other cultural practices, Travelers became
more hesitant to engage in discussion but were not yet acting embarrassed or proud. Their hesitations seemed to come from noticing
non-Travelers' reactions to their cultural practices and not yet understanding the reactions.

FIRST AND SECOND GRADES

These two grades will be discussed simultaneously because the
attitudes and behaviors of the children in both grades were so similar.
In first grade, there were 10 Travelers, 5 boys and 5 girls, out of 53
children. Travelers represented nearly 19% of the first-grade population. Two Travelers did not show up for school but had preregistered. In second grade, nearly 10%, or 5 out of 51 children, were
Irish Travelers. One preregistered Traveler never entered St. Jude.
There were four male Travelers and one female Traveler in second
grade.

The first- and second-grade teachers vary in ages from the mid-
twenties to early forties, with one teacher being a sister. One of the
lay teachers was new to the school and so had no prior experience or
knowledge of Irish Travelers, although she quickly learned certain
Traveler cultural practices from the kindergarten teachers.

Traveler children in first and second grades followed the same
pattern as the kindergartners in terms of entering school in late
October through mid-November.

Teachers and Parents

The interaction between Traveler parents and teachers decreased
significantly in the first and second grades. The majority of Traveler
children had attended St. Jude the year before and so were familiar
with the general atmosphere of the school. Teachers were prompt in
notifying Traveler parents if they believed a learning problem might
have been prevalent. Parents of these children kept in regular contact
with the teachers. After-school tutoring was a regular occurrence,

with Traveler mothers sending cash through the children rather than themselves coming into the classroom after school. Traveler children often carried $20 or more throughout the school day, without the teacher or other children knowing.

Most Traveler children, even in the upper grades, paid the teacher in the afternoon rather than in the morning for that day's tutoring session. One Traveler stated, "I don't know if I'll be here for tutoring. I may have to go home. I've been feeling bad this morning." Most of the time the student would attend the tutoring session even after a statement such as this. The same Traveler stated later that afternoon, after the teacher asked him why he didn't pay her in the morning, "Well, I don't like to pay for something ahead of time."

One Traveler mother, whose child was above average in her schoolwork, would nearly beg the teacher to tutor her. The teacher explained to the mother that her child did not need tutoring. The teacher believed the mother did not know how to react to a child doing well in school. Most Traveler mothers complain that they have an extremely difficult time, arguing with their children about coming to school. The teacher decided to get the mother more involved in the school so she could compare her child's academic performance with that of other children. The teacher asked the Traveler mother if she would help in the computer room once a week. The Traveler mother quickly replied, "I only went to eighth grade. I don't know nothing about computers." The teacher only responded, "You'll learn." The mother helped in the computer room at 8:00 a.m. every assigned computer day.

Teachers and Students

The first- and second-grade teachers are much more structured in their classrooms than those in kindergarten. Desks take the place of tables, and chairs are lined up in rows, facing one of the room's chalkboards, usually with the children's backs to the windows to avoid distractions. Only in one classroom were the desks frequently rearranged in various patterns.

The first- and second-grade teachers rarely spoke of Traveler children as a separate group. Most references were in conversations about a number of children, Travelers and non-Travelers. Many teachers in the upper grades, when discussing Traveler students specifically, would say the child's first and last name. There were numerous Travelers with the same first names so the use of the last names by teachers helped pinpoint exactly which Traveler was being discussed. Only one teacher out of the first- and second-grade teachers used the last names of two Travelers in her class in conversation. The teacher had two Traveler boys who were first cousins. One was very rowdy in class, and the teacher admitted she had a difficult time with him. He would start fights, call other children names, and use "dirty" language. The teacher believed he was very bright but totally disinterested in school. Parent contact did not solve the problem. The teacher would discuss the individual child's behavior without reference to the child being a Traveler.

Early Interactions

Through the use of sociograms, interviews, and observations, I found an increase in social integration between Travelers and non-Travelers and a slightly increased awareness by both groups of Irish Traveler ethnicity. With such a small number of Travelers in each classroom, asking the children to choose three classmates for the work and the play dimensions may have caused them to feel pressured to choose three even if they would prefer to limit their choices to one or two. Travelers often chose non-Travelers, however, for first and second choices in both dimensions. Travelers were selected as second and third choices by Travelers but never first. Rarely did a Traveler choose another Traveler for the work dimension. A student known to be bright was a common first choice among all the students for the work dimension.

Traveler boys were very interested in athletics and would play an organized ball game with non-Travelers at recess. This interaction was a positive influence on attitudes by both groups. Travelers were treated by non-Travelers as individuals rather than as a group. Family relationships were known by all, but relations did not necessarily form friendships at school. In three of the classrooms, Travelers were well integrated, although, in interviews, non-Travelers used the terms

Irish Traveler and *Gypsy* in discussing particular children—but usually not in a derogatory way. The exception was found when classmates discussed two cousins assigned to the same room. They were both male and the only Travelers in the room. One was the discipline-problem child of the classroom. He was constantly moving and talked out of turn in class. The following is a part of a conversation I held with a non-Traveler male student (NTS) near the middle of the school year about the teacher, Mrs. Ellen:

Me Does Mrs. Ellen have a favorite student?
NTS Not really. She likes everybody.
Me Really?
NTS Well, Tommy Costello is the worst kid in the class. Mrs. Ellen always has to tell him to sit down. He's always in trouble.
Me Do the boys play with him at recess?
NTS We've tried but he is mean. He and his cousin Patrick are always talking dirty.
Me Using curse words?
NTS Yeah [whispers] talking about body parts. They pick on everybody.
Me What do they do?
NTS They run by you and call you a name and kick you.
Me What does the teacher do?
NTS She makes them sit down near her but they keep doing it later.
Me Why do you think they act this way?
NTS I don't know. I guess because they are just mean.

Up to this point, the student never mentioned the term *Traveler*. He played with other Traveler boys from the other second-grade classroom with no conflicts.

Me Have you ever heard the word *Traveler*?
NTS Yeah.
Me What does it mean?
NTS The Gypsies.
Me And what are Gypsies?
NTS They are the cousins who live near each other and wear the same kinds of clothes.
Me How do you know all this?
NTS My mother used to teach here and told me. I also see them in church.
Me Are there any of these people at St. Jude?

NTS Yes! Tommy and Patrick in my class and Johnny and Joseph in the other class.

Me How do you know that?

NTS Because everybody told me.

Me Who told you?

NTS They were in my class last year and we knew.

Me Did your teacher tell you?

NTS No. I know because they are late for school and don't stay until school is through. They also look alike.

Me How do they look?

NTS The girls wear shiny things on their clothes and in their hair.

Me How about the boys?

NTS They just look alike and are cousins.

Me Why don't Tommy and Patrick play with Joseph and Johnny if they are all cousins?

NTS Because Tommy and Patrick are mean. Joseph and Johnny are good football players so they play with us. Tommy and Patrick probably can't play good so they make fun of us.

I also discussed Tommy and Patrick with Joseph and Johnny, who are both represented by a "T" in the following dialogue. The two boys mentioned the behavior problems Tommy and Patrick demonstrated at school and noted that their behavior was different at home.

Me Why don't Tommy and Patrick play with the others at recess?

T Because they don't like football.

Me So what do they do at recess?

T They run around.

Me They just run around?

T Yes. They kick people.

Me Do they do this to you?

T No.

Me Why not?

T Because I'd kick them back.

Me Why don't the other children kick them back?

T Some do but we aren't suppose to fight at school.

Me Would you fight with them at school if they kicked you?

T No. I'd get them at home.

Johnny and Joseph did not believe that they were responsible for Tommy and Patrick at school in their behavior with non-Travelers. They would explain that any retaliation on their part for the sake of non-Travelers would not be acceptable by other Travelers, even at this young age.

Tommy and Patrick, the only two Travelers in one classroom, chose each other first for the play dimension but chose popular non-Traveler children for the work dimension and for second and third places in the play dimension. They were not chosen by any non-Travelers.

One Traveler boy in another classroom was chosen as second by four non-Traveler boys in the play dimension. He was seen as a good athlete. This boy did not chose any Travelers for his list.

Later Interactions

There were no significant changes in the choices of Travelers and non-Travelers across the two groups. Changes in friendships were expected over the school year, and these changes were particularly seen in the play dimension. Tommy and Patrick, however, were still viewed as outcasts because of their behavior, choosing each other as first choice in both the work and the play dimensions.

Travelers in other classrooms were chosen by non-Travelers, and many choices complemented each other, showing an understanding and acceptance of the relationship between the children.

Although the Traveler boys who played with non-Travelers on the playground chose non-Travelers in the sociometric test, there was more interaction between the male Travelers toward the end of the year. Conversations began to develop between the boys concerning summer travel and leaving St. Jude. This minimal increase in inter-action among the Travelers did not alter the relationships with non-Travelers.

Close friendships were developing in school between Travelers and non-Travelers but the relationships were not encouraged in outside activities such as parties or sleep-overs. If a non-Traveler was planning a birthday party, he or she might send an invitation home to all the students in the classroom. The Traveler children never attended these functions. When Travelers had birthday parties, they were limited to family members or other Travelers and never included non-Travelers.

The Traveler children always said they were out with their parents and were unable to attend a non-Traveler function. Never was I told by Traveler children that they were not allowed to socialize with non-Travelers outside of the school setting. Non-Traveler students, in their conversations with me, were unaware of any boundary rules established by Travelers. The teachers in most of the classrooms tell parents and students that, if invitations or cards are to be distributed in class, all the children, or all one sex, must be recipients, sending a list home with each child of all the students. Any party that will be limited to a select few must be organized outside of school. This school practice encourages positive attitudes between Traveler and non-Traveler children, although non-Travelers are not yet aware that there is a pattern to the Travelers' lack of attendance at social activities. Rituals celebrated at school such as exchanging Valentine cards, bringing Halloween candy, or bringing a Christmas present for the teacher or another child are practiced by Travelers.

Absences

Among the first graders, the absences between classrooms were slightly different for the Travelers. Overall, the average number of days missed for classroom 1A was 5.77 (range = 0-13) while, for classroom 1B, the average was 6.29 (range = 0-15). Travelers missed an average of 3.2 days in room 1A (range = 1-5) and 7.4 days in room 1B (range = 2-15). The differences between Travelers in the classrooms were due to two students. One male missed 11 days and one female missed 15 days. Both of these students were the first two Travelers in first grade to withdraw from the school in May. Parents' attitudes toward school may have been the significant factor in the children's number of absences.

The first-grade teachers were very similar in teaching styles and discipline practices. From my observations and interviews, a large number of absences by Travelers could not be correlated with the teachers' behaviors. I must note that there were many non-Travelers who missed as many or more days than the Travelers in first grade.

The second grade shows a large increase in Traveler absences. The average absences for room 2A was 9.13 (range = 0-24.5), with

Travelers missing an average of 18.75 days. There were only two Travelers in room 2A, so the range is made up of their two totals—23.5 and 14 missed days. In room 2B, the class had an average of 6.92 days missed (range = 0-20), with Travelers having an average of 11.67 absences (range = 8-14). Discipline problems may account for the number of absences among Travelers in 2A. The teacher in 2A has a traditional teaching style in which teaching and learning are often restricted to textbooks and workbooks. The teacher in 2B often brought supplemental materials to class and assigned the students to research groups. In both classes, however, Travelers' absences nearly doubled the class average.

Summary of First and Second Grades

There were no changes in attitudes and behaviors of Travelers and non-Travelers during the school year in either first or second grade. The teachers did not focus on Traveler ethnicity when discussing academic or behavioral problems. There was at least one non-Traveler child in every classroom who required a considerable amount of contact with parents because of discipline problems. One child was expelled from St. Jude for constantly disrupting the class. In addition, there were numerous out-of-the-ordinary, overly concerned mothers who wanted parent-teacher conferences every day after school. With so many conflicts occurring, the Traveler children, if they were not discipline problems, were rarely noticed as different than non-Travelers. The large number of students in each classroom and the quantity of basic skills that must be covered may have caused many of the first- and second-grade teachers to overlook students' individual personalities and ethnic characteristics. Although individualized instruction was weakened, discriminatory practices based on ethnic or racial characteristics were rarely seen. The students were aware that their teachers treated everyone equally—unless a student was a discipline problem. This awareness by students contributed to the positive integration of Travelers and non-Travelers at these grade levels, also taking into account the influence of the developmental stages of ethnic socialization.

THIRD AND FOURTH GRADES

The two third-grade classrooms comprised 48 students with 3 male Travelers and 4 female Travelers. Nearly 15% of the third grade were Irish Travelers. All the students who preregistered were enrolled at St. Jude. In the fourth grade, there were 50 students with 16% Irish Travelers (5 males and 3 females). One male Traveler was pre-registered but did not enroll.

The teachers of the third and fourth grades were older, more experienced teachers than the majority found in other grade levels. Only one teacher was new to St. Jude that year but had taught for years in another Catholic school in the Diocese. The teachers' ages ranged from 27 to 62 with the average age being 42. The teachers, having been at St. Jude so long, knew most of the Traveler children, although most were unable to remember specific family relationships.

Travelers in these two grade levels had the earliest and latest dates for entering school. One Traveler in fourth grade entered on September 3, while another entered St. Jude on December 11. The Traveler entering in December had verification that she had previously been enrolled in another school that year.

Teachers and Parents

Traveler parents became more involved in the daily routine of their children by the third and fourth grades. They seemed to feel more confident in requesting homework or suggestions for their children. One teacher sent a note home to a Traveler parent and, the next afternoon, the mother visited the teacher. The teacher suggested that the mother have her son practice his multiplication tables in front of her. She willingly obliged but quickly added that she needed a completed multiplication table because she was not sure of all the answers. The teacher was not shocked but realized from her experience that she should have offered the multiplication tables before the Traveler mother had to ask and explain her request.

All the teachers at this grade level were aware of the educational level of the Traveler mothers and found that the mothers were quick to remind the teachers of their lack of formal education. Most Traveler mothers of elementary-aged children have only a third-grade education. To the teachers, a Traveler mother downplaying her intelligence is only a defense mechanism used to explain her child's academic deficiencies or lack of interest. When interviewed, one Traveler mother stated,

> Yeah, we tell the teachers how dumb we are because they think we are. If our children are doing bad in school, we go along with the teachers and play dumb. The teachers then can't say we don't know better. We admit our faults so it's up to the teacher to do something for our kids.

Another Traveler mother told me, "We know a lot more than they think we do but if we argue about it they will take us to be disrespectful and treat our children bad."

The teachers did not always remember that educational jargon is difficult for most parents to understand, especially those parents who have not experienced the educational system for very long.

A particular incident between a teacher and a Traveler mother and grandmother illustrates the potential conflict between teachers and Traveler parents. The teacher sent a note home to a Traveler mother concerning her child. The following afternoon, the mother and grandmother met with the teacher. The Traveler family had recently lost their father in an automobile accident and the boy's stuttering problem had increased. The teacher asked the mother if she had ever had her son tested. The mother quickly listed the number of medical doctors her son had seen. The teacher asked about seeing a psychologist and the mother started screaming that her son was not retarded. She ran out of the room, leaving the grandmother and the teacher behind. The teacher explained to the grandmother that she did not mean to suggest that the boy was retarded, instead, he was extremely bright, but the teacher was concerned with possible emotional problems the boy may be experiencing due to his father's death. The grandmother apologized and said she would explain everything to her daughter. No other reference to the incident was made in later conversations between the teacher and the mother.

At the stage of 8 and 9 years old, children become increasingly verbal in discussing school experiences at home. Children at this age are also aware of how to explain a school experience so their parents will go to the school in their defense. Traveler children are no exception. Although interaction between Traveler mothers and teachers increased in third and fourth grades, it was not limited to academic concerns. Many Traveler mothers complained to the principal and the teachers about discrimination their children experienced in dealing with non-Travelers, particularly in the use of the word *Gypsy*. One Traveler mother describes her dealings with her daughter in fourth grade in the following:

> These kids tell us mothers stories about how the country kids pick on them—calling them names and hitting them. They say they don't want to go to school no more because of the other kids. Some mothers give in to their kids and let them drop out or switch schools. I know better. My Margarite would complain every day that somebody was picking on her. I'd go down to the school and complain to the teacher. Finally, Margarite told me a girl named Ellen had called her a "Gypsy" and spit on her. I went down to the school so mad and found out that Ellen was absent that day. Margarite had made it all up. Now I ignore a lot of what she says. Sometimes I know it's true but she needs to learn to stand up for herself. I'm not gonna be around to take care of her all the time.

Traveler mothers did not hesitate to discuss their children's problems with the teachers or the principal. Early in the year, I removed Traveler children from one classroom for a short interview. They willingly provided their opinions of the school and began discussing their home life, with some probing on my part. The informal interview lasted approximately 20 minutes and I then removed a group of non-Travelers from the same classroom for a separate interview. The next day, one Traveler mother, saying she represented the other Traveler mothers, complained of my removing the Travelers from the classroom. She wanted to know what I was up to and why I was asking so many family questions. Sister explained that I was trying to understand the students' feelings toward school. The Traveler mother reminded Sister Catherine that, if Traveler children were continually isolated, they would be removed from St. Jude. After this incident, all other informal interviews were conducted outside of the structured classroom in natural settings such as the playground.

Teachers and Students

As students move into the third and fourth grades, they are being introduced to new skills but are also attempting mastery of skills presented in the earlier grades. The classroom structure in these classrooms was influenced by the age of the teacher and the number of years teaching. The older teachers were very traditional, with desks in rows facing the teacher's desk and teacher-directed lessons and group work reserved for reading. The younger teachers allowed more group work in all areas and encouraged group discussions.

In the earlier grades, teachers often discussed a student's ability level when discussing academic progress. In the third and fourth grades, the teachers began discussing academic problems in reference to an individual's motivation and interest in schoolwork. Third and fourth graders were perceived as more independent and as having a greater influence on their own academic performance. Third grade was the beginning of a loss of enthusiasm by many students toward school, and Travelers were no exception, showing a sharp decrease in interest at this grade level.

The teachers of the third and fourth grades often spoke of specific Traveler children and their academic or social problems. Primarily, the conversations centered on the high number of Traveler students' absences and the problem of helping them catch up.

The Traveler children at these grade levels often attended weddings and funerals with their parents. Younger children often stayed home with grandparents or aunts. Within five months, there were seven funerals, of which half were usually attended by the older children at St. Jude.

The 15 Travelers in third and fourth grades were not discipline problems. The girls would circle the teachers at recess to talk and in the classroom constantly volunteered to help. Although Traveler girls' interest in the teachers was unusual, their behaviors were not criticized. The main concern with the teachers was the lack of interest by many of the Traveler boys toward their schoolwork. The following was a conversation held by two teachers in the teachers' lounge concerning the problem:

Teacher 1 Tommy Riley does nothing in class. He won't even finish a worksheet that the other kids think is fun.
Teacher 2 Well you know [Travelers] will drop out before the eighth grade.
Teacher 1 So just pass them through? [No comment from Teacher 2, just a shrug of the shoulder.] I'm just amazed at how little education the mothers have. No wonder their kids do so poorly.
Teacher 2 Yeah. You can't expect much help from home when the parents don't even know third- and fourth-grade material. [The tone of voice of these two teachers was not one of disgust but one of despair.]

In the classrooms, the teachers did treat Travelers somewhat differently than non-Travelers. Teachers admitted to giving extra time to Traveler children to complete assignments or spending more time explaining directions. The majority of the third-grade Travelers were tutored after school but none of the fourth graders was tutored. The Travelers were not discipline problems. They were very quiet and polite in the classrooms. Although they often did not complete assignments, the teachers did not see this practice as creating a need for reprimand in front of the rest of the students, so often the other students were unaware that the Travelers were far behind in assignments.

Traveler and non-Traveler students felt that the teachers were fair in their treatment of students and had no favorites. Traveler children felt comfortable around their teachers and did not believe they were given any special attention. If the teachers spent extra time with a Traveler in the classroom, the Traveler believed that was expected behavior, not preferential treatment. Any problems the Travelers had outside of the classroom with non-Travelers were seen by the students as independent of the teachers.

Early Interactions

The Traveler children in third grade did not choose each other for first, second, or third places in the work dimension. Travelers understand the emphasis placed on grades by the school, and, being able to freely choose anyone with whom to work on a school project, they chose someone who does well in school to reduce the pressure placed on them to perform. The Travelers were not alone in choosing intelligent non-Traveler children for the work dimension, but they would overlook all the other Travelers, even the Travelers who were on the A honor roll, to choose non-Travelers. Travelers with high grades were also overlooked by non-Travelers in the work dimension.

For the play dimension, Travelers only chose Travelers for first choice. Non-Traveler isolates were the choice for second or third places among the Travelers, although on the playground the Travelers rarely played with non-Travelers. If a Traveler boy was the only Traveler boy in his classroom, he would play with the Traveler girls at recess or join other Traveler boys from other classrooms. Occasionally, the Traveler boys would join, without conflict, a ball game organized by non-Travelers. The four Traveler girls in third grade would organize their own games without involving additional classmates.

Fourth-grade Travelers chose other Travelers for the work dimension of the sociometric test. The Travelers' choices in the earlier grades were always similar to non-Travelers'; they chose the brightest student. The fourth-grade Traveler boys had a significant decrease in academic grades with the average grade a D. The girls were making Cs with one Traveler girl on the A honor roll. Grades, or pleasing the teachers, were no longer significant motives for Travelers in fourth grade. A preference for their own group was more important than accepting school values.

Non-Travelers did not choose Travelers in either area of the sociometric test in the early part of the year, and their reasons were often derogatory, referring to physical appearance or hygiene. Probing for further explanations, the non-Travelers would summarize their negative feelings by saying simply, "They are Gypsies."

The two groups did not interact positively or negatively on the playgrounds. The Travelers were beginning to be treated as outcasts by non-Traveler students, and they never confronted non-Travelers with their ascribed status.

The fourth-grade Travelers were very different than each other. One girl had high academic grades and discussed her dreams of becoming a psychologist. One boy had a stuttering problem but did well in academics. His social life among the Traveler children was very weak due to their perception of his handicap. The remaining Travelers were seen as "zombies" in class by the teachers and students. They never completed their assigned work, never participated in class discussions or showed enthusiasm toward anything related to schoolwork. The teachers and Travelers explained these attitudes and behaviors as resulting from plans for an early withdrawal from elementary school. The Travelers need only attend school for a specific number of years to satisfy their parents and they then join the adult world of work and marriage.

In the early part of the year, non-Travelers would speak of the Travelers who were not yet in school. Although the Traveler children were not known, personally, the last names and the fact that the children were not yet in school were enough clues to conclude they were Irish Travelers or, as often referred to, "Gypsies."

Later Interactions

Throughout the year, the separation between Traveler and non-Traveler students continued in both third and fourth grades. Non-Travelers did not choose Travelers for the play or work situations and most Travelers only chose Travelers, even selecting Travelers of the opposite sex. In the earlier grades, the children usually chose children of the same sex. If there were not enough Travelers to complete the list, non-Travelers of the same sex were chosen. By third and fourth grades, sex was often overlooked, especially in the work dimension.

By January, all of the non-Travelers referred to the Travelers as "Gypsies." Most of the third-grade non-Travelers had not heard the terms *Traveler* or *Irish Traveler*. The exceptions were the students who had brothers or sisters in the junior high grades. The children often overheard their older siblings calling the Travelers "nerds," "Gypsies," or "Travelers." Others noted that their parents criticized the Travelers' dress and behavior in church and in the larger community.

The Travelers in third and fourth grades were very well socialized into Traveler culture and would volunteer enormous amounts of data on their culture. In one conversation, one Traveler girl explained to me her general description of Irish Traveler culture:

Traveler We're Irish Travelers. We're different.
Me Different than whom?
Traveler From country people—that's what we call everybody who ain't Traveler.
Me How are you different?
Traveler Well, we only marry other Travelers and we get married young.
Me How young?
Traveler I know this girl last year that got married and she was 10. She dropped out of school after the fifth grade and got married.
Me Do you want to get married?
Traveler Yes! I'm gonna drop out after sixth grade and then get married to an older man.
Me How old do you want your husband to be?
Traveler About 20 or 21.
Me What about someone your own age?
Traveler No. You have to marry somebody who makes money and works a lot.
Me Do you want to live near your parents?
Traveler Yes, but we are all going to move soon. The airport is taking over our trailer park so we are moving. One man owns some land near here and we are all gonna move on it.
Me What do you want to be when you get older?
Traveler A housewife.
Me Wouldn't you like to do something exciting and different?
Traveler [laughs] No. I'll have children too and help my husband paint.
Me Is that what your mother does?
Traveler She goes shopping a lot and in the summer we go swimming and clean the apartment while my father and brothers are painting.

The Travelers in fourth grade often teased one Traveler boy throughout the school year. They made up a game in which you would have "Tommy disease" for 10 seconds if Tommy touched you or if you touched something Tommy just touched. Some of the non-Travelers would join in on the game in class but ignored the Travelers on the playground. One non-Traveler boy expressed his lack of understanding of the game. He thought the Travelers should not make fun of each other because they were cousins. He and most of the non-Travelers thought the game was insensitive because Tommy's cousins originated and generated the game.

Absences

The third-grade Travelers' number of absences was no different than the non-Travelers' average. In 3A, the non-Travelers' average was 7 days (range = 0-21) with the Travelers having an average of 7 absences (range = 6-8). In 3B, the Travelers had an average of 6.4 missed days (range = 2-9) and the non-Travelers' average was 6 absences (range = 0-12). The teachers were similar in their discipline techniques and teaching styles. There was a difference between teachers' ages and number of years of teaching experience but the Travelers' absences do not appear to have been affected by these differences.

Traveler mothers with children in third grade explained the reasons their children have fewer absences than those in the earlier grades. Traveler mothers still see 5-, 6-, and 7-year-olds as their "babies" and any whining or pains the Traveler children express are reasons to keep them home. At these ages, the mothers are able to continue their normal routines and bring their children along. By age 8, however, the Traveler children are more talkative and independent. An 8-year-old at home causes the mother to alter her routine for a child who may not be truly sick. Traveler mothers are not as patient and flexible with their children in terms of absences once they reach 8 years old. In addition, mothers realize the children may have only three more years of formal education and absences only reduce their knowledge base.

Whatever the Traveler mothers practiced for third graders to reduce absences, the same was not done for fourth graders. The average number of absences for non-Travelers in 4A was 5.4 (range = 1-10) with the Travelers missing 14.9 days of school (range = 4-29). In 4B, Travelers missed an average of 10 days (range = 6-15) and the non-Travelers' missed an average of 4.8 days (range = 0-15). The fourth graders with the lowest academic grades usually had the largest number of absences. During this school year, however, three of the Travelers contracted chicken pox, which accounted for at least five days of absences. Attendance at funerals or boys working with their fathers were two common excuses for absences. A funeral was often in another city, and the body was "kept on ice" until all family members were in town. The family would drive to the funeral and wait days for the ritual to begin.

Traveler men are constantly on the road to or from a job. If a small job is contracted for and the other brothers, brothers-in-law, or suitable family members are busy, a man may bring his young son for a four- or five-day weekend. The Traveler mothers do not discourage the practice because they believe their sons need the time with their fathers. There was a significant difference in the number of absences between Traveler girls and boys. The boys missed an average of 14.5 days and the Traveler girls missed an average of 9 days. The girls' excuses were explained as sick days while the boys were usually attending a funeral or working with their fathers.

One result of increased interaction between fathers and sons is an increased interest in dropping out of school. As the Traveler boys are given more responsibility in their fathers' jobs, it becomes more and more difficult for them to step backward in status to elementary school student. Traveler boys begin to resent the teachers, non-Traveler children, their mothers, and the concept of school because of the restraints. Traveler mothers begin to have more conflict at home with their sons by fourth grade over school attendance, which does not decline until the boys finally drop out of school.

Summary of Third and Fourth Grades

Traveler children in third and fourth grade had increased self-esteem in terms to their ethnicity. The only criticisms they had of non-Travelers was the use of the word *Gypsy*. Non-Traveler children did not solicit Travelers into their recess games or conversations nor did the Travelers try to increase interaction with non-Travelers. Accommodation was now being practiced by Irish Travelers in the third and fourth grades.

Ethnic awareness and own-group preference was well developed among Irish Travelers by third and fourth grades. Non-Travelers were aware of the differences between themselves and Travelers but did not interpret the differences as potential conflict as did the Travelers.

Teachers were not called to break up arguments involving name-calling between the two groups. These incidents occurred rarely, however. Name-calling was often a result of being quickly angered rather than of a premeditated plan to annoy another, and the children knew the difference.

Although conflict between Travelers and non-Travelers was minimal in the third and fourth grades, Traveler mothers' visits to the teachers concerning prejudice and discrimination increased due to the increased amount of conversations between the Traveler children and their mothers about school.

As Travelers' group preferences and ethnic awareness increased, they had more problems in accepting the school situation. How the Traveler child would respond to this growing conflict of interest was initially different with each individual. Each Traveler child was at a different level of internalizing ethnicity and potential conflict. The boys expressed conflict externally in the third and fourth grades, although in differing degrees, while the girls did not. There were differences between the two sexes but these may also be explained by the differences in socialization of Traveler boys and girls within Traveler culture in addition to differing levels of ethnic awareness.

FIFTH AND SIXTH GRADES

The fifth and sixth grades had so few Irish Travelers that the Travelers tended to exhibit similar behaviors and attitudes. There was only one Traveler in fifth grade, with each fifth-grade classroom having 22 students. In the sixth grade, there was one Traveler girl in each classroom, representing 4.4% of the classroom population. Only one Traveler for fifth and sixth grades did not enroll in St. Jude although preregistered.

Fifth grade was self-contained as were all the earlier grades. The teachers are in their fifties with nearly 20 years of teaching experience. One teacher, having the title of vice principal, did not have

Travelers in her classroom. With only one Traveler in fifth grade, the placement of this student was random, according to the secretary. This was the first year the vice principal could remember in which she did not have Traveler students. The teachers differed in their teaching styles. The vice principal was very traditional but had good rapport with her students. The other teacher would focus on social studies and incorporate all the other subject areas into a number of projects.

The sixth grade was the first time the students would experience both teachers for a grade level. In the earlier grades, the students had different teachers for art, music, physical education, and often religion, but all other subjects were taught by the one homeroom teacher. In the sixth grade, the teachers split the subject matter between themselves so that one taught reading and language arts while the other taught social studies, science, and math. The sixth-grade teachers were in their first year at St. Jude and in their first year teaching full-time. Both were flexible in terms of discipline and provided varied techniques for students' learning styles.

Teachers and Traveler Parents and Students

The fifth-grade teacher never met with her Traveler student's mother. The boy was making Bs and Cs in his subjects and his absences were not seen as a problem to either the teacher or the mother.

The mothers of the sixth-grade Traveler girls were very involved in field trips and class parties. The sixth-grade teachers were new and admitted they had no prior knowledge of Travelers so did not treat the Traveler students any differently than the others. The mothers did not use their group identity as an explanation for any academic problems their children may have experienced.

The positive relationship or lack of conflict between Traveler mothers and the teachers seemed to be related to the fact that only one Traveler was in a classroom. Without other Travelers, the student tended to integrate socially with non-Travelers, causing less prejudice and discrimination between the two groups to be exhibited and, finally, less chance of Traveler children complaining to their mothers about school.

The Traveler mothers of the sixth graders would offer to be chaperons for field trips and would allow non-Travelers to ride with them. When assigning students to cars, however, the sixth-grade teachers found that the non-Travelers often refused to ride in the "Gypsy car." Although the term *Gypsy* was rarely heard in the sixth-grade classrooms, the presence of a Traveler mother reminded the students of the Traveler culture. Elementary school-aged Travelers may be perceived as Irish Travelers only in some incidences but their mothers are the full representation of Traveler ethnicity. The sixth-grade teachers had to assign unpopular non-Travelers to the Travelers' cars. The Travelers knew what had occurred but did not press the issue. The Traveler mothers followed all the expectations of chaperons from disciplining the students when necessary to providing a side trip to a fast-food restaurant before returning to school.

The teachers believed Travelers offered to drive because they feared that the non-Traveler mothers would not carry their children. Also, Traveler mothers are very protective of their children and worry about their visiting a public place in which they may get lost or abducted.

Early Interactions

The fifth-grade Traveler, Gerard, was well liked by his classmates. He was never chosen for first place in the work dimension of the sociometric test but he was chosen by a number of students for second and third places. Gerard was chosen by two boys for first place in the play dimension and he chose these same boys for first and second choices for the work and play dimensions. Gerard never played alone at recess and would continue to play with his classmates even if fourth-grade Travelers were on the playground. He told me that the fourth graders were too young to play with at school but he did play with them at home.

Gerard had been at St. Jude for a number of years so the adjustment period was smooth once he entered in late October. The fifth-grade students knew what Gerard's family did in the summers and that he would be late in entering school. The boys seemed excited when he returned because he was seen as a good athlete with a good personality.

Although Gerard was well integrated into the social life of the classroom, he stated that he never visited his friends after school or talked to them on the phone. He never volunteered his phone number, and his friends never asked. He said that they probably knew he could not talk to them on the phone or meet them at the mall. Gerard said that his mother or sisters would not allow him to have any phone calls unless the caller was a Traveler. He had been told by his mother not to give out their phone number but to say they had no phone. Gerard wanted to be able to call his friends because he often forgot his homework assignments.

The two sixth-grade Traveler girls entered St. Jude the same week in early October. Margarite was new to St. Jude but Catherine had been attending St. Jude since fourth grade. Both were very quiet when they entered school and often spent their recess periods together. The principal had assigned them to separate sixth-grade classrooms.

The early sociometric tests showed that Catherine was chosen by two non-Traveler girls for the play and work dimensions. Catherine also chose these girls. Margarite chose popular girls for both dimensions but was only chosen by a non-Traveler isolate as third choice in the play dimension.

On the playground, Catherine joined the non-Traveler girls in conversations with Margarite standing nearby but not interacting. Some days, Margarite and Catherine would be alone at recess by their own choice.

The two Travelers had placed their orders for school uniforms but had not yet received them upon entering St. Jude. For two weeks, they wore dresses that characterized Irish Traveler style. The dresses were lined with sequins with shoes to match. The principal asked their mothers to downplay the elaborate outfits because they were a topic of conversation for non-Travelers.

Later Interactions

Gerard was chosen more often in the play dimension toward the end of the school year. His grades were good—Cs and Bs—so he was chosen by two boys for the work dimension. His friendship with his classmates continued to be limited to school, however. He did not complain about the limitations placed on him by his parents but felt they knew what was best for him. Gerard told me that his mother had said that country people should not be trusted: "They may be friendly on the outside but they talk about you behind your back." He did not believe his classmates were like that but stated, "I wouldn't be able to change my mother's mind. If I tried, she would get mad at me and then my father would get mad at me, so I just tell my friends that I don't have a phone."

The sixth-grade Travelers continued to have different relationships with non-Traveler students. Catherine was more outgoing and Margarite was more reserved and distant. When occasions arose that allowed the students to come out of uniform, Margarite and Catherine wore "Traveler" clothes. The students did not criticize the outfits but instead openly asked how the sequins were attached and how long it took to make the outfits. The Travelers were not embarrassed and volunteered answers. The outfits worn by the Travelers were of interest to non-Travelers but did not influence non-Travelers' clothes.

As the school year progressed, Margarite missed more school and became more disinterested in her schoolwork. She talked about entering the public school the following school year. Catherine's good grades and positive relationships with non-Travelers continued all year.

Absences

Gerard missed 25.5 days of school, but he was one of the few Travelers in the school to stay until the last school day in June. The average number of days missed by non-Travelers in Gerard's classroom was 6.6 (range = 0-24). Most of Gerard's absences were in the last six weeks of school in which his father had already left for the summer and his mother had stayed in town until school was out. The missed days were ones he spent with his father in Indiana.

In the sixth grade, Margarite missed 17 days of school, while the non-Traveler average was 7 absences (range = 0-19). In Catherine's class, the non-Traveler average was 5.8 absences and Catherine missed 3 days of school. The differences in the two girls' number of absences were due to the fact that Catherine was more socially integrated than Margarite in the sixth grade and Catherine's mother did not perceive this integration as a threat. Traveler girls do not help their fathers in their work so any absences were spent at home. Margarite told me that she would just say she didn't want to go to school and her mother would let her stay home. Catherine's mother was different. Catherine knew she could not fake an illness and she had to have a very good excuse for wanting to miss school. Catherine explained:

> I like school. The kids don't make fun of me so that makes things better. I want to go to high school so I have to go to school now. Margarite doesn't like school. She thinks everybody hates her. She just never talks to anybody. They think she's a snob when really she's just shy. She never studies so she will probably quit going to school after this year.

Summary of Fifth and Sixth Grades

The absence of conflict in the fifth and sixth grades was primarily due to the small number of Travelers in these grades. Without other Travelers in the same classroom, non-Travelers had to develop opinions on the individual rather than the group. A single individual has a better chance of being socially integrated into the classroom than an individual who identifies with a limited number of students in the classroom who share a reference group different than that of the rest of the class.

SEVENTH AND EIGHTH GRADES

In the seventh and eighth grades, there were four homeroom teachers who taught one or two subjects for both grade levels. Additional faculty would teach religion, art, music, library, and physical education.

There were 50 students in seventh grade, with a total of 6 Travelers (5 males and 1 female = 12%). At the beginning of the year, three Travelers were placed in one classroom and three in the other. After three weeks, one Traveler mother asked the principal to switch her son to the other homeroom to reduce discipline problems between two Traveler boys. When this happened, the Traveler distribution became four and two within the seventh-grade classrooms. One Traveler boy was preregistered but chose to enroll in the public school.

In the eighth grade, there was only one Traveler boy in a class of 25 students (4% of the classroom population). He had attended St. Jude for the past three years.

Three of the four seventh- and eighth-grade teachers were new to St. Jude but had an average of five years' previous teaching experience. Due in part to discipline problems the year before, St. Jude had lost most of the junior high teachers to other schools. Many students were not allowed to return so discipline the following year was not as much of a problem.

The Irish Travelers in the seventh grade were some of the latest to return to St. Jude. Four out of the six students entered St. Jude in November with one coming November 24. These four did show report cards from the schools they had attended in the beginning of the school year.

Teachers and Parents

All the parents of children in these two grades were very responsive to teachers' suggestions. Poor grades would quickly bring a parent or an older unmarried daughter to the school. Rather than blame the school or the teacher, the parents often explained academic deficiencies with reference to the laziness of their children. The Traveler mothers were very concerned about keeping their boys in school and expected them to show respect for the rules of the school. Although there was a significant amount of conflict between Travelers and non-Travelers in the seventh and eighth grades, the Traveler mothers did not become involved in the conflict. They believed their sons were nearly men and should learn to deal with the name-calling. The mothers would tell me they knew there was some fighting occurring at school between Travelers and non-Travelers but their sons did not talk about it very much at home because they would look like they could not stand up for themselves.

The main concern for Traveler mothers was whether or not their children would pass the grade. Tutoring was often used by Travelers at this grade level toward the end of each six-week period in hopes of raising the report card grade. The boys were more concerned about grades than the one Traveler girl. The boys felt pressure from home and were told they would finish the eighth grade if it took them 12 years. The only way out was to pass the classes because their mothers were serious about the issue. One Traveler mother, after a conference with the junior high teachers and the principal, stated:

> Johnny is going to graduate from eighth grade and go to high school. The way the painting business is now-a-days he may have to look somewhere else for a job and nobody will want somebody who didn't go to high school. He's just lazy. He can do it but I have to fight him about it all the time. He wants to be with his father painting. His father doesn't think Johnny needs to go to high school so I have that problem too. His father is not in town much so I have to make Johnny do his schoolwork all alone. I went only to the sixth grade and I have to read his books to help him. I think that if I can understand it from the book he should too. He was even in the class when the teacher went over it, so it shouldn't be as hard as he says. All his friends are dropping out of school and he wants to too but I say no. But I'm getting tired of fighting it. When he goes go to high school and flunks out, I won't be able to do anything. It's gonna be all up to him.

The frustration expressed by this mother was shared by all the Traveler mothers although most only hoped their sons would complete the eighth grade. High school was too much to expect for some. The Traveler girl's mother was not as concerned about her grades. Most Mississippi Traveler girls only go through the sixth grade so Sarah was going beyond the expectations of the group, although it was still an acceptable practice.

Sarah wanted to finish eighth grade although she knew she would probably be the only female Traveler in her classes. Her mother never visited the teacher but allowed Sarah to make her own decisions in terms of attendance and grades. Sarah never chose to be tutored.

Teachers and Students

The structure of the class schedule inhibited the teachers' teaching styles somewhat in that a class could not run into another class period. The students had to be ready to switch their focus with each teacher. The limitations in time resulted in a more traditional form of teaching to cover the required content. In addition, the principal believed the junior high age level needed more structure and discipline. The students were expected to be in their desks with enough work assigned to reduce discipline problems. One teacher referred jokingly to this age group as "walking hormones." To the teachers, many of the students were more interested in socializing than in studying. Most of the conflict between teachers and students was seen by the students as a result of the restrictions placed on them. The restrictions were not unusual but ones to help keep order in the classroom and on the school grounds. To the teachers, the junior high rebellion was seen as characteristic of the age rather than as a result of school rules.

In the seventh and eighth grades, conflict was prevalent between Travelers and teachers. The practice of not completing assignments was still prevalent among the Travelers, and the teachers would not let the students be overlooked. Reduction in time at recess, detention on Fridays, and parent-teacher conferences were all used to discipline students for unacceptable behavior. For the first time, teachers would reprimand the Travelers using their ethnicity in part of the conversations. Absences were also discussed in front of the entire class.

The junior high teachers felt that the existence of the Travelers in their classrooms only contributed to the potential conflict of the age group. The teachers did not perceive their behaviors toward Travelers as discriminatory, however, as did the students, but necessary to maintain order and reduce conflict. One example of conflict involved the Traveler boys disappearing from the playground at recess, later being found walking the halls in the junior high building. They were not involved in any destructive act but the fact that they had left the recess area without permission was enough for the teachers to get upset. The Travelers would continue to break this rule even when they might have been reprimanded two days before. The conflicts they had with the teachers only enhanced their disinterest in school.

Early Interactions

As roll was called in one seventh-grade classroom in the first two weeks of school, the students quickly explained to the teacher that the absent students were "Gypsies." The following was a conversation held in a seventh-grade classroom with the students explaining Irish Travelers to the new teacher:

Ted They all have the same names—Jim, Joe . . . If you went to the trailer park and called out Jim, they would all come out. They are mean too. One gypsy grabbed Mike around the neck last year in the bathroom for no reason. [The other students laughed and made comments that Mike encourages fights.]

Mike They are just a nuisance [referring to Irish Travelers].

Ted They say "J" or "G" to each other [referring to the nicknames used]. They steal and are Gypsies.

Mike They won't let four of them come into a store together because they will steal.

Ted They all have lice. Someone was sitting behind a Gypsy girl last year and saw all these lice in her hair.

During these comments, the rest of the class sat and listened without arguing. The new students were absorbing the information with shocked looks.

Ted If you went to the trailer park and yelled, "Free Paint" they would all run out! [The class laughs.]

Mike They are probably related to Sherwin Williams.

The class continued to laugh and the girls stated that the Travelers were not that bad. Ted was just trying to get everyone to laugh.

The new students at recess asked the teacher if they would be able to lock their belongings in the hall lockers before lunch to avoid the "Gypsies" stealing from them. Although the other students had a different perception of the Travelers than did Ted and Mike, the new students believed it all. The teacher explained the misconceptions and eased their concerns for the time.

The Travelers entered St. Jude between October 15 and November 24. All five boys in the seventh grade were new to St. Jude while Sarah had been at St. Jude since fourth grade. As the first boys entered separate classrooms, they were very obedient and polite and participated in class discussions but, as more Travelers enrolled, the Travelers' and non-Travelers' attitudes and behaviors changed.

The non-Travelers would ask the teachers the last names of the Travelers to verify Traveler ethnicity. When the first Traveler entered one classroom, the teacher told one non-Traveler that the new boy's name was Johnny Redmond instead of Johnny Riley. The non-Traveler boy could not believe that the new boy was not a Traveler but, when he heard the name Redmond, he believed the teacher. He was basing his belief on the boy's looks.

Word spread that Johnny's name was Redmond. Johnny did not hear the rumor for a few days. For those few days, Johnny was escorted to lunch by a group of boys, offered a seat at their lunch table, and chosen for a football team at recess. Only until another Traveler enrolled and Johnny began a conversation with him did the non-Travelers ask him his last name. Once the name Riley was heard, the non-Travelers changed their behaviors. The presence of another Traveler also changed Johnny's behavior. The two boys wanted to sit alone at lunch and play alone at recess. Johnny immediately changed his attitude toward his schoolwork and the non-Traveler students. As the remaining four Travelers entered St. Jude, the division between Travelers and non-Travelers increased.

In the cafeteria, the seventh graders were assigned to one set of tables and the eighth graders to another set of tables. There was only one Traveler in the eighth grade and the other eighth graders refused to sit with him. The teachers tried assigning seats so that he would also have students at his table but the friction was so strong that he asked if he could sit with the seventh-grade Traveler boys. The seventh-grade Traveler boys sat at one table and Sarah sat with the non-Traveler girls (boys and girls were separated). The request was granted and, throughout the year, the eighth-grade Traveler sat on the seventh-grade side of the cafeteria.

The special request was not questioned by any non-Travelers because they knew what discrimination the Travelers experienced and the request would not threaten them. Sarah declined to sit with the Traveler boys because no other girl sat with boys.

Sarah engaged in conversation about schoolwork at lunch but was not included when the students discussed parties. On the playground, Sarah stayed with the Traveler boys.

On the first sociometric test, the seventh-grade Travelers chose only other Travelers for both the play and the work dimensions. This was the first time Travelers were closed to non-Travelers on a sociometric test. The non-Travelers were also closed, as they never chose Travelers in either dimension. The sociometric test correlated with behaviors inside and outside the classroom. In the eighth grade, the one Traveler was forced to choose non-Travelers. His choices were students who were very open-minded and somewhat less discriminating than the others. Two out of the three he chose were girls. These students did not choose the Traveler, however.

Later Interactions

As the school year progressed, most of the students developed stronger friendships and became more judgmental of others. The Travelers were totally isolated and constantly in conflict with non-Traveler students. Non-Travelers, usually boys, complained that the Traveler boys would start fights, be given special attention by teachers and the principal, and were allowed to be socially promoted.

The teachers were more lenient on the Travelers in terms of assignments because of the decreasing interest the students showed toward school. The Travelers were reprimanded in front of the class for incomplete work just as the other students but sometimes a Traveler's completed assignment was graded more subjectively than the non-Traveler's work. The teachers believed a few good grades would motivate some to work harder. The strategy worked for a short period but many of the Traveler boys would return to their old behaviors. One Traveler explained:

I only have one more year then I say, "Good riddens school!" I'm gonna help my father paint and if painting is slow then I'll lay linoleum. I don't need school. I'll do just enough to pass this grade. You have to be pretty stupid not to pass a grade. I ain't that stupid!

The Traveler boys were often in the principal's office for fighting with non-Travelers and each other. One Traveler boy would corner another boy every day in the classroom or on the playground, pushing the student up against a wall with his chest, waiting for the student to strike first. This Traveler would choose anyone with whom to start a fight.

The 12- and 13-year-old boys are at a period in which their honor must be protected. The most easygoing non-Traveler student when confronted with a fight cannot easily retreat without losing face, especially if the fight is encouraged by an Irish Traveler. The same feelings are held by Travelers as non-Travelers.

The majority of the Traveler boys were passive but would not discourage the more aggressive ones. Instead, any accusations made by a Traveler were supported by the other Travelers and any accusations made toward a Traveler by a non-Traveler were also defended by other Travelers. The group cohesiveness of the Travelers was perceived by non-Travelers as justification for their own attitudes and behaviors toward the group.

After a number of arguments on the playground between Traveler and non-Traveler boys, the principal called one of the Traveler boys into her office. The principal asked the boy why the Travelers would not play with the other boys. The boy began crying, telling the principal that he wanted to be friends with the others but he could not. "If I make friends with country people then I won't have any friends in the trailer park. They will make fun of me and fight with me." The principal then realized the strong attachment the Traveler children have to their culture.

Sociometric tests constructed later in the year showed no change in the division between Travelers and non-Travelers in the seventh grade. Travelers continued to choose Travelers, and non-Travelers continued to choose non-Travelers. The eighth-grade Traveler continued to choose friendly non-Travelers although no one chose him.

The teachers allowed the seventh-grade Travelers to work together on research projects. If a teacher attempted to integrate the Travelers with non-Travelers, the Travelers would either refuse to do the assignment or become so involved in arguments because they were not contributing to the group that the teachers felt that, by allowing Travelers to work together, the classroom climate would be more conducive to learning.

The eighth-grade Traveler would be assigned to the most open-minded students. The students knew the Traveler, Pete, had to be assigned to a group, so resistance was useless.

Absences

In the seventh grade, the Travelers had an average of 10.3 days missed (range = 6-18). The non-Travelers missed an average of 5.6 days (range = 0-21) in 7A and 4.8 days (range = 0-18.5) in 7B. Sarah missed the most number of days among the Travelers. She would be absent for most major test days and field trip days. The Travelers who were involved in fighting at school would miss more days than the passive Traveler boys.

The Travelers knew they could miss up to 29 days without being automatically retained, but their mothers would not allow them to skip school very easily. Many times, a Traveler boy would come to school with a bad cough and the mother would only drop off cough drops rather than take him home. The mothers said it was a constant battle getting their sons in junior high to be interested in completing the eighth grade.

Pete, the eighth-grade Traveler, did not miss one day of school. He entered St. Jude at the end of October and stayed until the end of school. He even participated in the eighth-grade graduation and returned to school for an additional week of supplemental work requested by his mother. His mother stayed in town with him while he completed his schoolwork. The average number of absences for his eighth-grade class was 8.3 (range = 0-27). Pete's mother was instrumental in sending him to school and making sure he completed the eighth grade. There were approximately three Traveler boys in eighth grade in the public schools so Pete's educational level was unusual among his Traveler cohorts.

Summary of Seventh and Eighth Grades

The significant variables for the increase in student conflict seem to be the combination of age, sex, and the large number of Travelers in seventh grade. The age of junior high students is one of changing personalities and bodies. Boys tend to be developmentally less advanced than girls. Emotions are more difficult to suppress. Potential conflict surrounds this age and, when an ethnic group is included in the classroom in which differences in attitudes and behaviors exist, the conflict surfaces. The students are at an age in which they are trying to understand themselves in the context of their reference group. Irish Travelers must go through the same identity process. Each group evaluates the norms as presented by their reference group. Travelers and non-Travelers have some differences in norms because of their different groups. The existence of differences is often perceived as threatening to identity.

The fighting that occurred in the junior high over trivial things was a symbol of defending one's social identity. By fighting, the Travelers were showing their loyalty to their ethnicity. Non-Travelers engaged in fighting Travelers because Travelers did not represent their reference group. The conflict between Travelers and non-Travelers at these grade levels demonstrates the crystallization of ethnic awareness and identity.

6

Discussion of Results

This chapter will discuss the patterns of interactions outlined in the previous chapter. Following the same sequence as in Chapter 5, the interactions will be analyzed for all nine grade levels: teachers and Traveler parents, teachers and students, Traveler and non-Traveler students, and absences. Finally, an overview of the development of ethnic attitudes will be presented focusing on the influence of the school setting.

TEACHERS AND TRAVELER PARENTS

The Traveler mother, not the father, is responsible for the child's school education. Traveler mothers show great interest in their children's education at all grade levels but the types of interaction between teachers and mothers differ.

In kindergarten, Traveler mothers and sometimes grandmothers were in constant contact with the teachers, but, by first and second grades, contact was limited to the emergence of academic problems. Tutoring was still encouraged throughout the primary grades but the mothers no longer interacted with the teachers on a daily basis. For example, in kindergarten, a Traveler mother would pay the teacher, directly, for tutoring after the session. By first and second grades, the child, after the tutoring session, would collect the money from the mother in the car and return to the school building to pay the teacher. An alternative to this was to allow the child to carry the cost of the one day's tutoring or one week's tutoring to school in the morning and pay the teacher in the afternoon. Traveler children would not pay the teacher in the morning because they believed there was always a chance that they might become sick in the middle of the day and go home, in addition to the practice of not paying for services in advance.

Most non-Traveler mothers would ask the teacher after a tutoring session about the child's progress for that day. These mothers believed they were entitled to a progress report because the cost of tutoring was an expense in addition to school tuition. The non-Traveler mothers were very money conscious and acknowledged these feelings to the teachers. Travelers acted as if they had full trust in the teachers' abilities at tutoring, however. Any tutoring cost was interpreted as the answer to obtaining passing grades. Traveler mothers believed, or allowed teachers to believe, that "the teacher knows best." As discussed in the previous chapter, tutoring was also used by Traveler mothers to shift the potential blame from them to the teachers—tutoring was an accommodating practice to reduce conflict between Travelers and school administrators.

Interaction between Traveler mothers and teachers increased in third and fourth grades due to the development of ethnic awareness and own-group preference by both Traveler and non-Traveler children. For the first time in school, the children were learning what it meant to be an Irish Traveler, and preliminary attitudes were forming based on limited knowledge and interaction. The preliminary attitudes could be positive or negative, depending upon the interpretation of the acquired knowledge and interaction. The resulting behaviors or reactions to the interpretations could be ones of conflict or lack of conflict.

Traveler mothers would contact the teachers in hopes of reducing the conflict between Travelers and non-Travelers. The conflict was minimal but it was the foundation for future actions and attitudes.

From fifth grade to eighth grade, contact between Traveler mothers and teachers was very limited. Notes sent to Traveler mothers by teachers explaining an academic or social problem usually resulted in a note returned assuring the teacher that appropriate discipline had been administered at home. If a teacher asked a Traveler mother to meet with her after school, the mother would attend or send the oldest unmarried daughter.

Traveler mothers mildly defended their daughters' low grades but were very confident that their sons would improve their grades with some social restrictions at home. Traveler mothers demonstrated a wide gap between valuing education for sons versus daughters.

TEACHERS AND STUDENTS

Teachers in kindergarten through second grade did not perceive discipline problems as related to ethnicity. Although the Traveler children in kindergarten, first grade, and second grade were on the edge of developing preliminary ethnic affiliation, their behaviors were not due to conflict with non-Travelers or teachers. The teachers were aware of Traveler culture but did not define each child as a product of Traveler culture. Social or academic problems encountered were not blamed on the Traveler way of life but on the individual circumstances.

This individualistic approach used by the teachers was transferred to their students, who, at a low level of ethnic attitude development, discussed single Traveler children's behaviors in terms of the child and not the family background.

As the children began developing stronger attitudes toward Traveler ethnicity in the third through the eighth grades, the teachers also began labeling students as Travelers. Traveler children's ethnic preference was viewed by non-Traveler students and teachers as a threat to the status quo. Negative attitudes held by teachers and non-Travelers began to emerge due to conflict.

The teachers who did not discuss Travelers' culture in a negative way all viewed the conflict between Traveler and non-Traveler students as negative but unavoidable due to the existence of two varying ethnic groups.

The most "open-minded" teachers in the upper grades still resorted to labeling Traveler children as "Travelers" when discussing social or academic problems. In these upper grades, ethnicity was considered by the teachers to be so salient among the Travelers that it was the "cause" of all problems Traveler children experienced in the school. No longer were Traveler children viewed individually but, instead, as products of their culture.

All the teachers held similar knowledge of Traveler culture but the quality of interaction differed with each grade level. The teachers had all developed ethnic attitudes toward Irish Travelers but the different interaction patterns between Traveler and non-Traveler children in the school influenced teacher behaviors. If teachers at any grade level experienced conflict, their immediate behavior was to reduce the conflict for the specific time and place.

To the junior high students, both Travelers and non-Travelers, the teachers' reactions were often interpreted as discrimination toward Travelers, when, from the teachers' perspectives, they were only trying to reduce conflict and maintain order. The expected behavior within the school, however, is that of non-Traveler culture. The teachers' behaviors toward Travelers did influence the students' behaviors and attitudes but, as one views the entire school population, conflict between Traveler and non-Traveler children occurred before teacher and Traveler conflict. Teacher-Traveler conflict usually developed as a result of Traveler/non-Traveler student conflict.

STUDENTS' INTERACTIONS

In general, Travelers socialized with Travelers at recess and were not chosen by non-Travelers in the work or play dimensions of a sociometric test. The only exceptions were in fifth and sixth grades, in which there were so few Travelers that their reference group during school time was that of non-Travelers. In first and second grades, Traveler boys did play with non-Traveler boys at recess but the friendships were limited to school activities. Generally, throughout the nine grades, Traveler girls played only with other Travelers—boys and girls.

On the sociometric test, Travelers chose non-Travelers with high grades for the work dimension just as did non-Travelers, but the two groups generally picked their own group members in the play dimension. The three Travelers in the fifth and sixth grades had to choose non-Travelers in both dimensions because of the lack of other Travelers to complete the list. Their choices do not necessarily reflect their attitudes toward non-Travelers but illustrate one limitation of the use of sociometric tests.

The increase in years of schooling among Irish Travelers contributes to an increase in knowledge of and interaction with students from various backgrounds. As students begin to develop their own-group preferences, criticism of others increases as a means of self-defense and self-awareness. Travelers and non-Travelers experience the same developmental stages of self-awareness and own-group preference but at different rates.

The two groups experienced conflict due to their choices of group affiliation. Boys tend to express conflict more than girls. Part of the explanation are the shared sex role socialization patterns emphasized in both Traveler and non-Traveler cultures. Non-Traveler and Traveler girls did not express any feelings of threat to their identity with the presence of the other group. Girls did discriminate but, when interviewed, the prejudice was not evident—at least not as strongly as with the boys. Girls tended to show discrimination because segregation of the groups was expected behavior. Non-Traveler girls could not explain the origin of the segregation, however. Traveler girls, as early as third grade, stated that they learned of the expected segregation at home and the purpose was to prevent marriages between the two groups.

ABSENCES

Traveler students demonstrated a higher number of absences compared with non-Traveler absences, and the number of absences increased with each grade level (excluding eighth grade). No student at St. Jude missed a large number of days due to an unusual illness or injury. The absences given in Table 5.1 include unexcused and excused absences taken from the attendance register given to the school office at the end of the school year.

The two teachers for each grade level in the kindergarten and first- and second-grade classrooms were dissimilar in the way they structured their classrooms. The higher number of absences for all students in the lower grades was found in the highly structured, traditional classrooms. From third grade to eighth grade, the teaching styles and classroom structure did not appear to influence the absentee rate.

Non-Traveler girls usually missed more school than non-Traveler boys throughout most of the grades. The reverse was true, however, for Traveler students in third and fourth grades.

Conflict at school between Traveler and non-Traveler students was not a predictor of Traveler absences. Individual circumstances influenced many Traveler absences, such as a father needing his son for itinerant work, expected attendance at a funeral, or a lenient mother. Some Traveler mothers even encouraged their children's absences if the children's school experiences were "too positive." For example, when asked why her son missed so many days of school, one Traveler mother stated:

> Gerard comes home and is always talking about his "friends" at school. These friends he's talking about is country people. We don't want our kids hanging around country people. I'm glad he's making good grades but I don't like him with those country kids—so when he doesn't want to wake up early some mornings, I let him sleep. Then it's too late to go to school. He doesn't want to go in the middle so I just say he can go in the next day. Some days he wants to go even if he's late and I bring him even if I don't want to. I don't want him telling his teacher that I won't bring him to school.

Attitudes such as the ones just described help explain why some Traveler students, who seem semi-integrated with non-Travelers and experience little conflict at school, have the largest number of absences.

The eighth-grade Traveler boy was never absent from school. There was no real difference between his school experiences and those of other Travelers, but his grade level and his mother's control over him may have been the most influential factors. Few Mississippi Travelers reach the eighth grade and this particular Traveler mother wanted her son to go to high school. She knew he needed as much out of St. Jude as possible for success in high school. The boy told me that all his friends were already working with their fathers, so attending school provided a means to pass the time. He was friendly with the seventh-grade Travelers and viewed school as a social setting even though conflict was present.

Although each Traveler had his or her own explanations for absences, most of their excuses were related to their disinterest in formal education, lenient mothers, and funeral attendance. Travelers did not believe that the school setting and its requirements played a significant part in influencing their absences. Mississippi Travelers would not allow school to interfere with their cultural practices.

DEVELOPMENT OF ETHNIC ATTITUDES

Ethnic attitudes have usually been described as developing through a series of stages (Goodman 1964; Aboud 1977) in which each person progresses but at different ages. Figure 6.1 presents my perception of the development of ethnic attitudes at St. Jude. Travelers and non-Travelers follow the same sequence of stages, with information and interaction steadily increasing and influencing the stages.

The first stage, "Unawareness of Differences," is seen in the early part of kindergarten and by all new students and teachers in the beginning of the school year.

As interaction between Travelers and non-Travelers increases, so does knowledge helping development of awareness of differences. The non-Travelers may move into this stage from the previous stage within days while others develop throughout the school year.

Becoming aware of one's group affiliation occurs after differences are defined. The child or teacher begins to compare Traveler and non-Traveler characteristics and is able to identify with one group in Figure 6.1 more than the other. Travelers move into this stage more rapidly than non-Travelers due to their minority/marginal status in the larger community. Ethnic awareness is emphasized at home by such things as conversations discussing "those country people."

Once a child or teacher identifies with one group, attitudes begin to develop toward the other group. I refer to these attitudes as preliminary attitudes because they are very weakly founded and susceptible

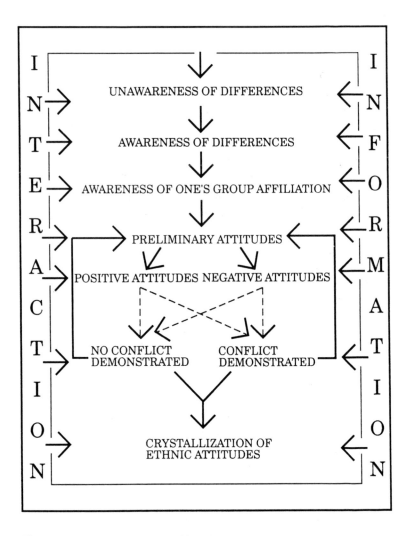

Figure 6.1. The Development of Ethnic Attitudes

to change. Preliminary attitudes may be either positive or negative due to information gathered or quality of interaction. In addition, the positive or negative attitudes do not necessarily elicit conflict.

Merton (1976) describes four types of behaviors when discussing prejudice and discrimination: (a) prejudiced discriminator, (b) prejudiced nondiscriminator, (c) nonprejudiced discriminator, and (d) nonprejudiced nondiscriminator. Attitudes (i.e., prejudice) do not always predict behavior (i.e., discrimination), so dashed lines are used in Figure 6.1 between attitudes and behaviors.

The outcome of these attitudes and behaviors helps form stronger (crystallized) attitudes that are less likely to change. Some attitudes are so primitive, however, that the behaviors and the reactions to the behaviors revise the preliminary attitudes. Only when the revisions are consistently accepted for all situations will they be "crystallized."

Additional information and interaction do not guarantee a change in ethnic attitudes that have "crystallized." For example, by seventh and eighth grades, most of the students' attitudes, especially among males, are "crystallized." Trying to sway male seventh and eighth graders' attitudes concerning Traveler and non-Traveler cultures was nearly impossible.

TRAVELER ETHNICITY AND THE SCHOOL

Travelers are categorized as students at St. Jude but they are not full participants. Their culture does not include school as a major social institution but a place in which one spends time to avoid legal actions. Formal education is not valued in other areas of their cultural practices such as itinerant work or marriage arrangements. Too much formal education can produce negative consequences because it requires more interaction with non-Travelers, especially for the girls. For example, a Traveler boy will not marry a girl with more education than he, so a desire for education beyond the seventh grade would be detrimental to a Traveler girl's future.

The teaching styles and classroom structures do not appear to be significant factors in the academic or social achievement of Traveler children.

Overall, Traveler children appear to be well adjusted in their culture and are beginning to show signs of decreased dependency on non-Travelers except for economic purposes. Traveler culture provides the necessary elements to maintain its membership.

Although Travelers may be referred to as a pariah or a marginal group, they do not demonstrate a resistance to the separation between themselves and non-Travelers. Instead, Travelers encourage the continual segregation for the sake of maintaining their ethnicity.

Georgia Travelers' educational practices are different than those of Mississippi Travelers. The difference is not due to their culture but to the influence the church administrators have on the Traveler community in Georgia. Georgia Travelers have a high attendance rate in the Catholic school in which they are enrolled. The pastor and school principal have taken legal action to ensure that Traveler parents enroll their children in school. The community in which the Georgia Travelers reside was organized by a non-Traveler priest, who helped construct a Catholic church for the Travelers in the community. The parish priests assigned to the church over time have been strong agents of change and control. For example, community parties are decided upon by the priest; marriages must be approved by the priest; and elaborate church attire is discouraged by the priest. Although the priests have been influential in the Georgia Traveler community, the Travelers often ignore their requests. The philosophy of the earlier priests was assimilation of Travelers into the mainstream society.

Mississippi Travelers often refer to the circumstances of the Georgia Travelers. The Mississippi Travelers do not want church intervention in their community because they realize they would have to give up some of their cultural practices. Mississippi Travelers have a closer-knit community and stronger boundary rules than the Georgia Travelers.

In dealing with Mississippi Travelers, any disagreement at school can result in a Traveler child being removed by the mother. Traveler mothers are not willing to allow the school to be more of a socializing agent than the family. Although disagreements in school may upset a Traveler mother, the lack of conflict is seen more as a threat. As long as Traveler and non-Traveler children disagree, the boundary rules are in place and ethnicity is maintained. If the children ignore the boundary rules, ethnicity begins to lose its salience and importance. Traveler mothers place more value on their ethnicity than on formal education.

St. Jude's teachers generally understand the Travelers' way of thinking although they do not all believe it is "right." The biggest complaint among the teachers toward Traveler culture is the lack of choice the young Travelers have in terms of career aspirations. The overall philosophy of teachers toward Traveler children is expressed by one teacher:

> They have been Travelers for decades. Why would they want to change now? Instead of trying to change them, just try to educate them as much as possible for the short time they are with us. Each generation goes to school a little longer. Maybe they will all finish eighth grade in the future—but they will still be Irish Travelers. Education won't change that.

7

Summary and Conclusions

In studying the macro and micro levels of interaction at St. Jude, I was able to examine Irish Travelers' school experiences. In addition, I was able to examine the external, cultural factors that set the tone for the interaction patterns within the school setting. Focusing on the initial questions raised in the Introduction, I will briefly summarize my findings for each.

WHEN DO CHILDREN DEVELOP THEIR ETHNIC AWARENESS?

Once in the field, I learned of varying levels of ethnic awareness held by Traveler and non-Traveler children and adults that contributed to the quality of interaction between the two groups. From my 10 months in the field, I developed a flowchart (Figure 6.1) illustrating the developmental stages that all children and adults, non-Travelers and Travelers, at St. Jude appear to follow in developing their ethnic attitudes toward Traveler ethnicity.

Traveler children demonstrated an awareness of their own ethnicity before non-Traveler children did. The saliency of Traveler ethnicity did not influence non-Traveler attitudes until non-Travelers were developmentally ready to interpret the Traveler characteristics as distinct Traveler characteristics. Once non-Travelers were aware of Traveler ethnicity, an increase in the saliency of Traveler characteristics influenced the rate of the development of preliminary attitudes toward Travelers.

HOW DO OTHERS INFLUENCE THE
DEVELOPMENT OF A CHILD'S
ETHNIC AWARENESS?

Among the Travelers, the family or cultural group is still the main social institution for socialization. The interaction opportunities that are provided by the school setting, however, help Traveler children become more aware of their ethnicity and provide a means by which to practice the group's boundary rules.

Most non-Traveler children learned of Traveler ethnicity primarily through peers, then through immediate family, and finally through teachers. Non-Traveler teachers were "educated" by other teachers and their own students. Of course, all the participants increased their knowledge through interaction.

HOW DO ETHNIC AWARENESS AND
SALIENCY CONTRIBUTE TO PREJUDICE
AND DISCRIMINATION?

Traveler ethnic saliency does not guarantee ethnic awareness by non-Travelers. Only when a non-Traveler has developed an awareness of Travelers is saliency identifiable. For example, a Traveler girl may wear sequins on her school uniform, which is characteristic of Travelers, but, until a non-Traveler associates sequins with Travelers, the presence of sequins will not be acted upon by the non-Traveler.

As ethnic awareness is developed, Irish Traveler saliency is identifiable and, as a result, positive or negative attitudes form toward Travelers and non-Travelers. The types of attitudes, in addition to the social surroundings, influence the child's interaction through behavior that is based on discrimination or nondiscrimination. An increase in saliency of Travelers as preliminary attitudes are forming encourages a person to revise these attitudes or crystallize ones already held.

An ethnic group that holds values different than the dominant group is seen as a threat to the status quo. The school is society's only institution in which every child must participate. The school is society's institution that teaches society's rules and values. If the school doesn't teach the child, society may never have another chance with that child, so conformity is an underlying principle of formal education.

Irish Traveler saliency is a reminder to society and to St. Jude that Travelers have not conformed. I must emphasize that conformity is not synonymous with assimilation. St. Jude accepts the fact that Travelers will never assimilate but are expected to acculturate. Acculturation may be expressed as a change in cultural patterns demonstrating a gradual movement toward assimilation. Acculturation would show signs of conformity. By this definition, Travelers do not show signs of acculturation.

As discussed earlier, Travelers are an accommodating group. They only hide their ethnicity to reduce conflict but never to delete conflict. Without conflict, their boundary rules are unimportant.

WHAT IMPACT DOES ETHNIC AWARENESS HAVE ON THE SCHOOL SETTING?

WHAT IMPACT DOES THE SCHOOL HAVE ON ETHNIC AWARENESS?

The presence of Travelers greatly influences the school setting. Teachers must adjust their lessons to help the Travelers catch up after missing two months of school in addition to the large number of absences within the school year. Racial tensions between other minority students and Whites are generally absent and this fact may possibly be due to the presence of common scapegoats—Irish Travelers. The presence of Travelers also allows teachers to earn extra money for after-school tutoring of Traveler children. Finally, with ethnic diversity at St. Jude, Travelers are given the opportunity to defend their ethnicity, which in turn reinforces Traveler beliefs and boundary rules.

The school provides a place in which interaction between Traveler and non-Traveler children is accelerated. Without the school, Traveler and non-Traveler children may not have acted upon each other's ethnic status due to a lack of awareness of differences and a decrease in the chance of direct interaction.

The ethnic awareness and ethnic attitudes that develop by way of the school are not a result of the school curriculum but of the school's physical and social structures. The phrase "in this world but not of this world" describes the Travelers at St. Jude School. They are enrolled in the school but are not full participants because they do not accept the basic goals of society's formal educational system.

TRAVELERS AS INFORMANTS

Many small minority groups that have a history of prejudice and discrimination by the majority group develop strong boundary rules. One boundary rule often practiced is avoiding telling the whole truth to an outsider. Travelers use this practice regularly with non-Travelers. It provides a shield of protection against further discrimination and helps to maintain traditions or practices identified as belonging to Traveler culture, such as the existence of their Cant or Traveler family life.

In my research, I found that Travelers, whether adults or children, offer different responses depending upon the social context of the conversation. For example, if I asked the same Traveler student three different times what he did on Halloween night, he would often give me three different answers depending on whether we were alone, in front of the entire class, or with other Traveler students.

During the 10 months in the field, I had to consider the social context of my interviewing to determine the truth. As Traveler children developed their ethnic attitudes, their responses had to be carefully analyzed for they were learning the Traveler adult way of communicating with non-Travelers.

WHAT IS THE FUTURE FOR
TRAVELER CHILDREN IN THE SCHOOL?

A pluralistic society may be described as one in which a number of ethnic or racial groups coexist with a minimal amount of conflict and with a general acceptance of each other's differences. The situation that exists at St. Jude and within the outside community is not one of pluralism.

Irish Traveler history has been one of marginal status as horse and mule traders. This marginal status influenced the development of an ethnic identity. The emergence of an ethnic identity included a well-defined set of boundary rules to separate Travelers from non-Travelers. As time progressed and Travelers remained itinerant, stereotypes held by both groups toward each other increased as a sign of group loyalty. Travelers may even speak of their group to non-Travelers using some of the stereotypes originally devised by non-Travelers. Reinforcing non-Travelers' stereotypes ensures the distance the Travelers prefer between the two groups.

Travelers continue to maintain the status held by marginal peoples as described by Park (1950, p. 67): "They occupy a place somewhere between the more primitive and tribally organized and the urban populations of our modern cities, they may be called 'marginal peoples.' " Other examples of marginal peoples described by Park include the Acadians of southern Louisiana, the Mennonites, and the Whites of Appalachia. The term *pariah* is often used with certain minority groups, such as Gypsies, but the Travelers do not fit the definition of *pariahs*: "any person of a degraded or despised class; a social outcast" (*Oxford English Dictionary* 1961, p. 477). Travelers may have their conflicts at St. Jude but they provide needed and often welcomed skills to the outside community. They are full participants in the economic structure of the country even though itinerancy is not highly respected. Travelers have chosen to forfeit respect in non-Traveler social circles to provide services that contribute to their economic status among their own group. At St. Jude, the administration views the Travelers as needed, paying students in a parish that has an unstable budget.

The itinerant aspect of Traveler culture is one of the threads that holds the group together. Only when Travelers become settled will Traveler culture be greatly altered. From past adaptation practices, abandonment of the itinerant life-style appears to be very unlikely for the Travelers. Schools that enroll Irish Travelers must be willing to work with children whose families do not accept the dominant culture's values toward education, and the schools should not have any expectation of changing those values. Mississippi Travelers do not want special programs such as migrant programs or special schools. Georgia Travelers have experienced "special treatment" and, as a result, boundary rules are often broken, with an increase in non-Traveler and Traveler marriages.

Mississippi Irish Travelers have been Travelers for more than 100 years and the culture is very much alive. To Travelers, some conflict in the school will only benefit the maintenance of their culture.

SUMMARY

In most educational research, recommendations are expected. The question arises, "Recommendations for whom—the school, the Travelers, or other researchers?" Although I am a product of the educational system, I am also a researcher who aims for objectivity. Providing recommendations for one group would only show biases. Attempting to be an outsider and observing Travelers at St. Jude, I saw an accommodating group that has "put up" with non-Travelers' requests for some formal education. The values toward formal education have not been incorporated into Traveler culture although there has been an increase in school years completed over the generations. To Travelers, school experiences up to the sixth grade are not a threat to ethnicity. Their frequent decisions to remove their children after sixth grade are because of the increased threat to maintaining their ethnicity after that time. The six years of education has been an increase over the previous generation but Travelers are not yet willing to risk their children's ethnicity for additional formal education.

Schools that enroll Traveler children are not always the important factor in Traveler's decisions to stay or drop out of school. Travelers know society is changing, and children are more knowledgeable about such topics as world affairs and sexual practices. This increase in knowledge is a result not only of the school but also of societal changes, such as increased communication with parents, the media, and access to more reading materials.

This increase in what Travelers call the "maturity" of non-Travelers, and not the school curriculum, is the concern of Traveler mothers. The school is the institution in which society groups children, however, and, as a result, Traveler children must interact and will therefore learn from non-Traveler children.

Traveler children tell their parents about the topics they hear about from non-Travelers. The knowledge that non-Traveler children hold frightens Traveler mothers because such topics are not discussed in Traveler culture or are reserved for adult conversations. Traveler mothers believe that the consequences of the physical and social conditions of formal education are too detrimental to Traveler culture.

Schools cannot easily change society or inhibit societal influences. Discussions in the classrooms can be monitored, but they cannot be on the recess grounds or in the rest rooms. Traveler children will be exposed to all sorts of topics while they are students in school.

The Amish have the same concerns as do Traveler parents. As a result, courts have allowed the Amish to set up their own schools. Travelers have not yet expressed this desire.

In dealing with an accommodating group, schools must consider the positive consequences of the ethnic group. Among Irish Travelers, some of the positive characteristics include (a) that the parents are very involved and concerned about the child's education and welfare; (b) family values are very strong and traditional; (c) the extended family is still an important factor in the culture; (d) parents believe the birth of children is an asset rather than a liability; (e) there are no divorces within the community; (f) members feel strong bonds to the group; and (g) the group provides services for its members.

Does the school want to assimilate a group that does not want to assimilate? Does society have that right? Obviously, with the Amish, society has decided that the Amish have the right to maintain their cultural practices. They are not viewed as a threat to the dominant group, and they hold traditional values that are still valued but less practiced in our larger society.

One of the problems lies with the fact that schools are designed to teach the values of the dominant group. Pluralism has yet to be fully practiced in the school systems.

Travelers will need to be the ones to take the initiative to change the educational system in which they enroll their children. Travelers do not trust non-Traveler laypeople. Although a layperson may have good intentions, Travelers believe there are underlying plans for assimilating their children. A clergy member is more trusted than a layperson by the Travelers and will need to be the one to act as liaison between the Travelers and the school system.

Changes in educational practices among Mississippi Travelers will be very slow due to the influence the church has on the Georgia Travelers. Distrust even of clergy members about education is still high among Mississippi Travelers. Time and the increased involvement of Traveler mothers in the school may change educational values and practices.

Societal influences on non-Traveler children will not decrease, so Travelers must decide whether they will take more risks by increasing their children's formal education, help to organize Traveler-only classrooms, or continue to withdraw their children from school before high school.

This research was not conducted to provide answers for St. Jude or for Traveler parents. My goal was to present the social consequences of the presence of an accommodating group such as Irish Travelers in one school. With this information, Travelers and school personnel are better able to make decisions for the future by interpreting the present. Researchers in ethnic studies should reevaluate traditional theories of ethnicity by taking into account the existence of accommodating groups and the functional role that conflict may hold in maintaining ethnicity for certain types of ethnic groups, such as those who have chosen to accommodate rather than acculturate.

References

Aboud, Frances E. 1977. "Interest in Ethnic Information: A Cross-Cultural Developmental Study." *Canadian Journal of Behavioral Science* 9:134-46.

———. 1984. "Social and Cognitive Bases of Ethnic Identity Constancy." *Journal of Genetic Psychology* 145:217-29.

———. 1987. "The Development of Ethnic Self-Identification and Attitudes." Pp. 32-55 in *Children's Ethnic Socialization: Pluralism and Development,* edited by Jean S. Phinney and Mary J. Rotheram. Newbury Park, CA: Sage.

Amidon, Edmund J. and Ned A. Flanders. 1963. *The Role of the Teacher in the Classroom.* Minneapolis: Paul S. Amidon.

Andereck, Mary E. 1988. "Irish Travelers in a Catholic Elementary School." Ph.D. dissertation, Texas A&M University, College Station.

Anderson, Harold H. 1939. "The Measurement of Domination and of Socially Integration Behavior in Teachers' Contacts with Children." *Child Development* 10:73-89.

Asher, S. R. and V. L. Allen. 1969. "Racial Preference and Social Comparison Processes." *Journal of Social Issues* 25:157-67.

Barth, F. 1969. *Ethnic Groups and Boundaries.* London: George Allen and Unwin.

Bogdan, Robert and Steven J. Taylor. 1975. *Introduction to Qualitative Research Methods.* New York: John Wiley.

Byrd, Eugene. 1946. "A Study of Validity and Constancy of Choices in a Sociometric Test." *Sociometry* 14:175-81.

Caldwell, Edson. 1959. *Creating Better Social Climate in the Classroom Through Sociometric Techniques.* San Francisco: Fearon.

Clark, A., D. Hocevar, and M. H. Dembo. 1980. "The Role of Cognitive Development in Children's Explanations and Preferences for Skin Color." *Developmental Psychology* 16:332-39.

Clark, K. B. and M. P. Clark. 1939. "The Development of Consciousness of Self and the Emergence of Racial Identification in Negro Preschool Children." *Journal of Social Psychology* 10:591-99.

———. 1947. "Racial Identification and Preference in Negro Children." In *Readings in Social Psychology,* edited by T. M. Newcomb and E. L. Hartley. New York: Holt.

Cogan, M. L. 1956. "Theory and Design of a Study of Teacher-Pupil Interaction." *The Harvard Educational Review* 26:315-42.

Cooley, Charles H. [1902] 1964. *Human Nature and the Social Order.* New York: Schocken.

129

Denton, Nina P. 1983. "A Community in Learning: An Ethnographic Description of Classroom Interaction." Ph.D. dissertation, Arizona State University.

Denzin, Norman K. 1978. *The Research Act: A Theoretical Introduction to Sociological Methods.* 2nd ed. New York: McGraw-Hill.

Dewey, John. [1938] 1968. *Experience and Education.* New York: Collier.

Epstein, Y. M., E. Krupat, and C. Obudho. 1976. "Clean Is Beautiful: Identification and Preference as a Function of Race and Cleanliness." *Journal of Social Issues* 32:109-18.

Fine, M. and C. Bowers. 1984. "Racial Self-identification: The Effects of Social History and Gender." *Journal of Applied Social Psychology* 14:136-46.

Fox, D. J. and V. D. Jordan. 1973. "Racial Preference and Identification of Black, American Chinese, and White Children." *Genetic Psychology Monographs* 88:229-86.

Francis, E. K. 1976. *Interethnic Relations: An Essay in Sociological Theory.* New York: Elsevier.

Geertz, Clifford. 1973. *The Interpretation of Cultures.* New York: Basic Books.

Genessee, F., G. R. Tucker, and W. E. Lambert. 1978. "The Development of Ethnic Identity and Ethnic Role-Taking Skills in Children from Different School Settings." *International Journal of Psychology* 13:39-57.

George, D. M. and R. A. Hoppe. 1979. "Racial Identification Preference and Self-Concept." *Journal of Cross-Cultural Psychology* 10:85-100.

Georgia General Assembly. "Taxation." Part I, Title II, Paragraph 56, p. 73, in *Acts and Resolutions of the General Assembly of the State of Georgia 1927.* Atlanta: Author.

Glazer, Barney G. and Anselm L. Strauss. 1967. *The Discovery of Grounded Theory: Strategies for Qualitative Research.* Chicago: Aldine.

Gmelch, George. 1985. "The Cross-Channel Migration of Irish Travelers." *Economic and Social Review* 16(4):287-96.

Gmelch, Sharon. 1975. *Tinkers and Travellers.* Dublin: D. O'Brien.

Goffman, Erving. 1961. *Asylums.* Garden City, NY: Doubleday.

Goodman, M. E. 1964. *Race Awareness in Young Children.* New York: Collier.

Gordon, Milton M. 1964. *Assimilation in American Life: The Role of Race, Religion, and National Origins.* New York: Oxford University Press.

Greeley, Andrew M. 1974. *Ethnicity in the United States.* New York: John Wiley.

———. 1977. *The American Catholic: A Social Portrait.* New York: Basic Books.

Greeley, Andrew M., William C. McCready, and Gary Theison. 1980. *Ethnic Drinking Subcultures.* New York: J. F. Bergin.

Griffin, John H. 1962. *Black Like Me.* Boston: Houghton Mifflin.

Gronlund, Norman E. 1959. *Sociometry in the Classroom.* New York: Harper.

Guba, Egon. 1981. "Criteria for Assessing the Trustworthiness of Naturalistic Inquiries." *ERIC/ECTJ Annual Review Paper* (March).

Harper, Jared V. 1969. *Irish Traveler Cant: An Historical, Structural, and Sociolinguistic Study of an Argot.* M.A. thesis, University of Georgia, Athens.

———. 1977. "The Irish Travelers of Georgia." Ph.D. dissertation, University of Georgia, Athens.

Hraba, J. and G. Grant. 1970. "Black Is Beautiful: A Reexamination of Racial Preference and Identification." *Journal of Personality and Social Psychology* 16:398-402.

Isajiw, Wsevolod. 1974. "Definitions of Ethnicity." *Ethnicity* 1:111-24.

Katz, P. A. 1976. "The Acquisition of Racial Attitudes in Children." In *Towards the Elimination of Racism*, edited by P. A. Katz. New York: Pergamon.

Kircher, M. and L. Furby. 1971. "Racial Preferences in Young Children." *Child Development* 42:2076-78.

Landreth, C. and B. C. Johnson. 1953. "Young Children's Responses to a Picture and Inset Test Designed to Reveal Reactions to Persons of Different Skin Color." *Child Development* 24:63-79.

Liebow, Elliot, 1967. *Tally's Corner*. Boston: Little, Brown.

Martin, James G. and Clyde W. Franklin. 1973. *Minority Group Relations*. Columbus, OH: Charles E. Merrill.

Mays, V. M. 1986. "Identity Development of Black Americans: The Role of History and the Importance of Ethnicity." *American Journal of Psychotherapy* 40:583-93.

Mead, George H. [1934] 1966. *Mind, Self and Society*. Chicago: University of Chicago Press.

Merton, Robert K. 1976. "Discrimination and the American Creed." Pp. 189-216 in *Sociological Ambivalence and Other Essays*. New York: Free Press.

Mindel, Charles H. and Robert W. Habenstein, eds. 1978. *Ethnic Families in America: Patterns and Variations*. New York: Elsevier.

Moreno, J. L. 1934. *Who Shall Survive?* Beacon, NY: Beacon House.

Oxford English Dictionary. 1961. Oxford: Clarendon.

Park, Robert E. [1925] 1967. *The City*. Chicago: University of Chicago Press.

———. 1950 (posthumous). *Race and Culture*. Glencoe, IL: Free Press.

Phinney, Jean S. and M. J. Rotheram, eds. 1987. *Children's Ethnic Socialization: Pluralism and Development*. Newbury Park, CA: Sage.

Piaget, J. 1954. *The Construction of Reality in the Child*. New York: Basic Books.

Porter, J. D. R. 1971. *Black Child, White Child: The Development of Racial Attitudes*. Cambridge, MA: Harvard University Press.

Powell-Hopson, Darlene and Derek S. Hopson. 1988. "Implications of Doll Color Preferences Among Black Preschool Children and White Preschool Children." *Journal of Black Psychology* 14:57-63.

Ramsey, Patricia A. 1987. "Young Children's Thinking About Ethnic Differences." Pp. 56-72 in *Children's Ethnic Socialization*, edited by Jean S. Phinney and Mary Jane Rotheram. Newbury Park, CA: Sage.

Ranking, D. Fearon. 1891. "A Family of Shelta-Speaking and Romani-Speaking Highland Tinkers." *Journal of the Gypsy Lore Society* (First series) 2(5):319-20.

Rice, A. S., R. A. Ruiz, and A. M. Padilla. 1974. "Person Perception, Self-Identity, and Ethnic Group Preference in Anglo, Black and Chicano Preschool and Third-Grade Children." *Journal of Cross-Cultural Psychology* 5:100-108.

Rosenfeld, Gerry. 1971. *"Shut Those Thick Lips!" A Study of Slum School Failure*. New York: Holt, Rinehart & Winston.

Rotheram, M. J. and Jean S. Phinney, eds. 1987. "Introduction: Definitions and Perspectives in the Study of Children's Ethnic Socialization." Pp. 10-28 in *Children's Ethnic Socialization: Pluralism and Development*. Newbury Park, CA: Sage.

Royce, Anya Peterson. 1982. *Ethnic Identity: Strategies of Diversity*. Bloomington: Indiana University Press.

Schwartz, Howard and Jerry Jacobs. 1979. *Qualitative Sociology: A Method to the Madness.* New York: Free Press.

Sinclair, John McHardy and Richard M. Coulthard. 1975. *Towards an Analysis of Discourse: The English Used by Teachers and Pupils.* London: Oxford University Press.

Spencer, Margaret B. 1982. "Personal and Group Identity of Black Children: An Alternative Synthesis." *Genetic Psychology Monographs* 106:59-84.

————. 1984. "Black Children's Race Awareness, Racial Attitudes and Self-Concept: A Reinterpretation." *Journal of Child Psychology and Psychiatry* 25:433-41.

————. 1985. "Cultural Cognition and Social Cognition as Identity Correlates of Black Children's Personal-Social Development." In *Beginnings: The Social and Affective Development of Black Children,* edited by M. B. Spencer, G. K. Brookins, and W. R. Allan. Hillsdale, NJ: Lawrence Erlbaum.

Spradley, James P. 1979. *The Ethnographic Interview.* New York: Holt, Rinehart & Winston.

————. 1980. *Participant Observation.* New York: Holt, Rinehart & Winston.

Spradley, James P. and Brenda Mann. 1975. *The Cocktail Waitress: Women's Work in a Male World.* New York: John Wiley.

Stevenson, H. W. and N. G. Stevenson. 1960. "Social Interaction in an Interracial Nursery School." *Genetic Psychology Monographs* 61:37-75.

Theodorson, George A. and Achilles G. Theodorson. 1969. *A Modern Dictionary of Sociology.* New York: Harper & Row.

Thomas, W. I. [1931] 1966. "The Relation of Research to the Social Process." Pp. 289-305 in *W. I. Thomas on Social Organization and Social Personality,* edited by Morris Janowitz. Chicago: University of Chicago Press.

U.S. Bureau of the Census. 1982. "Users' Guide." Part B. Glossary. Pp. 37-39 in *1980 Census of Population and Housing.* Washington, DC: Government Printing Office.

U.S. Bureau of the Census. 1990. "Content Determination Reports." No. 6 in *Census of Population and Housing.* Washington, DC: Government Printing Office.

Williams, J. E., D. L. Best, and D. A. Boswell. 1975. "The Measurement of Children's Racial Attitudes in the Early School Years." *Child Development* 46:494-500.

Withall, John. 1949. "The Development of a Technique for the Measurement of Socio-Emotional Climate in Classrooms." *Journal of Experimental Education* 17:347-61.

Wolf, R. L. and B. Tymitz. 1977. "Ethnography and Reading; Matching Inquiry Mode to Process." *Reading Research Quarterly* 12.

Wright, Don. 1981. "Beware the 'Gypsy' Trailer Scam." *Trailer Life,* July, pp. 12-14.

Zinser, O., M. C. Rich, and R. C. Bailey. 1981. "Sharing Behavior and Racial Preference in Children." *Motivation and Emotion* 65:179-87.

Index

Aboud, F. E., 4, 14, 15
Absences from school, 67, 76, 86, 92, 101, 109-111
Accommodation
   definition of, 3
   use of, 5, 37, 121, 124, 126
Acculturation
   definition of, 3, 121
Alcohol, 33
Allen, V. L., 15
Amidon, E. J., 49
Amish, 125
Andereck, M. E., 5, 21
Andersen, R., 42
Anderson, H. H., 49
Anglo conformity, 12
Asher, S. R., 15
Assimilation
   definition of, 3, 11-12
Attitude crystallization, 14, 112, 113

Bailey, R. C., 15
Best, D. L., 15
Bogdan, R., 47
Boswell, D. A., 15
Boundary rules, 3
Bowers, C., 17
Byrd, E., 50

Caldwell, E., 52
Cant, 21, 37, 69
Clark, A., 15
Clark, K. B., 15
Clark, M. P., 15

Cogan, M. L., 49
Confirmation, sacrament of, 31
Cooley, C. H., 47
Coulthard, R. M., 49
Cultural pluralism, 12

Dembo, M. H., 15
Denton, N. P., 50
Denzin, N. K., 13
Dewey, J., 47

Eighth grade, 93-102
Engagements, 27
Epstein, Y. M., 15
Ethnic group, 12
Ethnic identity, 13, 87, 106
Ethnic socialization, 13, 17, 87, 120
Ethnicity
   definitions of, 9, 10
Ethnogenesis, 12
Ethnography, 48

Family structure, 27
Fifth grade, 88-93
Fine, M., 17
First communion or First Eucharist, 31
First grade, 70-77
Flanders, N. A., 49
Formal schooling, 35, 109
Fourth grade, 78-88
Fox, D. J., 15
Francis, E. K., 10
Franklin, C. W., 10

135

About the Author

Mary E. Andereck is currently employed as a principal at Cathedral Grade School, a Catholic school, in Memphis, Tennessee. She received her Ph.D. in Curriculum and Instruction from Texas A&M University in 1988, with an emphasis in the sociology of education. Her M.A. is from Indiana University with a major in comparative and international education and a minor in Latin American studies (1980). Her undergraduate degree is in elementary education from Louisiana State University (1976). She has taught at both the elementary school level and the university level. Her research and teaching interests include the sociology of education, minority/ethnic groups, ethnic socialization, family studies, and qualitative methodology.